Liter

Other Pocket Essentials by this author:

Georges Simenon

Literary Theory

David Carter

www.pocketessentials.com

This edition published in 2006 by Pocket Essentials
P.O.Box 394, Harpenden, Herts, AL5 1XJ
www.pocketessentials.com

A CIP catalogue record for this book is available from the British Library.

ISBN 1 904048 66 8
EAN 978 1 904048 66 4

2 4 6 8 10 9 7 5 3 1

Typeset by Avocet Typeset, Chilton, Aylesbury, Bucks
Printed and bound in Great Britain by Cox & Wyman, Reading

For Kim Chan Young and his family

Acknowledgements

The debt to other scholars is enormous, but there is simply no scope within the confines of this modest volume to acknowledge them all. The authors of the works included in the section of Reference Material are owed the greatest debt: I frequently compared my opinions with theirs and checked for general agreement on factual details. On the personal level I have greatly appreciated discussions with Kim Chan Young, well read in the field, and Kim Duk Yung, a sociologist. I have also consulted students for their opinions on the usefulness and accessibility of available books on literary theory. Finally I would like to record here the seminal influence on my own thinking about literature of my 'Doktorvater', Dr. Hans Popper, one of that rare breed, which I allude to in my introduction, who made me think seriously about the nature of literature long before it became fashionable to speak of 'literary theory.'

Contents

Introduction

Attitudes to the study of literature have undergone nothing short of a revolution in the last half-century or so. Changes were afoot in the previous half-century but they moved at nothing like the pace and in nothing like the variety of ways that have been evident since the Second World War. It is true that writers and critics had been reflecting on the nature of literature at least since Aristotle but, in the course of the twentieth century, the whole concept of a 'literary text' became questionable.

As a student of European literature in the 1960s I heard little mention by my professors of 'literary theory.' Genre (tragedy, the novel, the sonnet etc) was certainly mentioned and so were the writer and the critic, but any allusion to the reader was rare indeed. Everyone talked freely of the writer's 'intention' and the 'meaning' of the text. When it was deemed necessary, one brought in consideration of the writer's 'background', the 'historical context', and the 'philosophical climate'. There was also such a thing as 'practical criticism', which literature departments made their students do, although no-one explained to us why we had to do it, or how it would be useful to us in our studies. It was assumed that its usefulness was obvious. You took a sample of an unfamiliar text, translated it, if necessary, pointed out a few significant figures of speech that you recognised, such as a metaphor or a simile, discussed its meanings and implications, brought in a bit of background knowledge, if you had any, and that was about it. If you did this well under exam conditions, you passed the exam, proving to all who cared to know that you could analyse literature. There were the great writers and the not so great writers and, by heeding one's professors, one gradually learned to distinguish them. Occasionally, one heard of a 'psychoanalytic interpretation' or a 'Marxist approach', but, more often than not, they were mentioned in a tone that suggested that these were slightly disreputable activities. If you were lucky, you might be blessed with one lecturer who was open to new ideas and challenges. Then, suddenly, when I was a postgraduate in the late 1960s, all these keen young lecturers appeared telling us that our very notion of a 'literary text' was questionable. Whole edifices of carefully constructed bodies of knowledge started to shake at the foundations. Nothing was sure or sacred anymore. It was becoming difficult to utter a word of comment on anything, especially literary works, without justifying yourself theoretically. Naturally the question arose, 'Why do we need theory?' Hadn't we been managing quite well without it, thank you very much, for some considerable time?

Why Theory?

What professors, teachers and lesser mortals did not realise, or were reluctant to admit, was that, in fact, they had been using theory all their adult life, without knowing it (rather as Monsieur Jourdain in Molière's play *Le Bourgeois Gentilhomme* does not realise, until it is pointed out to him, that he has been speaking prose all his life). How could this be? Quite simply because there is 'live theory' (theory we consciously consider when making judgements) and 'dead theory' (the theory which lies behind the assumptions we hold when making judgements but which has become so integrated into our common practice that we are no longer aware of it). Many had been discussing literature using 'dead theory', without having bothered to analyse their own presuppositions. So the answer to the question 'Why theory?' is quite simple: because it is better and more honest to be aware of the reasons why you do something than to be ignorant of them. If this maxim holds good for all human endeavours, then there is no reason why the study of literature should be exempt from it.

The problem is that defining what counts as 'theory' and what one means by 'literary' is no easy task. Most critics and theorists have grappled bravely with the problem but have finally given up, declaring that it does not matter anyway. Some theorists lead one to the conclusion that literary theory does not really exist as an independent discipline. There is, many claim, just 'Theory', theory about everything from literature to lesbianism, from hooliganism to horror films. Since many books are to be found with the phrases 'Literary Theory' or 'Theory of Literature' in their titles, however, it is clear that there is a body of thought to which the terms can be applied. There is a kind of theory with literature as its focus. This is an important fact to establish, because there are other kinds of theory, such as 'Critical Theory' and 'Cultural Theory', which rely on the same theorists and schools of thought as 'Literary Theory'. The difference between them all is clearly one of focus and attention. The theorists and schools of thought considered in this book have in common the fact that they challenge 'common sense' notions of what literature is. They often question our assumptions about 'great literature' and propose different ways to analyse and evaluate it. However, any vague statement about literature (such as 'All literature is escapist') does not constitute a theory. It must meet more stringent requirements to be considered both valuable and valid.

What Counts as Theory?

Clearly, in the first instance, a theory must attempt to explain something. Its proponents may believe that it does this successfully but others may not. Jonathan Culler, an eminent populariser of literary theory, has made a useful distinction: '...to count as a theory, not only must an explanation not be obvious; it should involve a certain complexity' (Culler, 1997). Unfortunately, many theorists have not only recognised this basic truth but have taken it too passionately to heart, cloaking their insights in obscure language. Yet it is clearly true that new understanding often comes only after developing a model of some complexity in the mind. Literature, in all its forms, treats of human life, its nature and problems, its mode of existence, its ways of coexistence and thought, and its belief systems. Any theory about these phenomena can, therefore, be considered relevant to the study of literature. However, the actual application of such theories is a complex procedure, fraught with pitfalls, to which the revered academic, as much as the novice scholar, is disturbingly liable to succumb. Misinterpretation, false analogy, unfounded generalisation, reductive argument – all these hazards lie in wait for the unsuspecting critic. It is also, therefore, in the nature of theory that not only does it have some complexity but that it is also often difficult to prove or disprove. A theory may sound very convincing but can it be proved to have validity? If it cannot be proved, does it thereby lose its usefulness? And what would constitute proof, or disproof, of any given theory? Does it finally matter whether it can be proved or not? These are questions which it is difficult enough to answer in the fields of the so-called natural sciences and in sociology, psychology and other disciplines. What of literary theory? It would seem wise to consider first exactly what the object of study is.

What is Literature?

Because many theorists have been primarily concerned with phenomena other than literature (psychoanalysts with the human mind, Marxists with human existence in a capitalist society etc), it has often been of only secondary importance to them whether a text they are considering can be deemed to be literary or not. Often the same methodology is applied in analysing texts, which may resemble each other in many ways, but which must be identified differently. One can imagine, for example, one text which is a short story told in the first person, taking the form of a confession to a murder, and another text which is an actual signed confession by a real murderer. They might be almost identical in language, structure and content. The important difference is, of course, that the reader knows that one is a story and the other a real confession, and judges them accordingly. In the case of the story, the reader might consider whether or not it was realistic or whether or not the character was telling the truth, but would not need to question whether or not it was an authentic document, written by the person named. In the case of the real confession, it would be possible, in principle, to check its truth content against known facts. This would not be possible, nor would it be relevant in the case of the story. The reader thinks this way because he or she knows that the story is a literary text. But how is it obvious that the text has a quality which we call 'literariness'?

It would seem that a definition of 'literariness' should be of urgent concern. Yet the authors of books on literary theory provide no such adequate definition. This is likely to be due to the nature of language as much as to the incompetence of theorists. The lack of a definition, which could be applied to all works regarded as literature, is not necessarily a bad thing. Many of the most useful words, in all languages, are useful precisely because they do not designate something very specific, but identify a range of meanings and related phenomena. Where would we be without such words as 'Love', 'Hate', 'Work', 'Business', and, more pertinently, 'Music', 'Drama', 'Art', etc? All the things which we might group together and to which we might apply one of these words bear family resemblances to each other, but they are also all highly individual. If we had to have words for every single experience, we would not be able to communicate with each other about those experiences. We need words, such as 'literature' and 'literary', indicating such family resemblances, to enable us to communicate information about individual differences to each other. All attempts at defining literature therefore have proved to be only partial and thus of little practical use: the best that has been thought and said; language taken out of context; language organised in a special way which distinguishes it from its other uses; language used to create a fictional world. None of these definitions is close to being adequate or useful, because none of them refers exclusively to literary language (a mentally ill person, for example, can also create a fictional world).

The words 'literature' and 'literary' have also changed their meaning over time. Before about 1800 literature meant all kinds of writing, including history and philosophy, and it is possible to trace the gradual shifts in meaning all the way up to the present. This all leads to an inevitable conclusion: that literature is what a given society at a given time considers it to be. This may not be a very useful conclusion, but it is certainly true, and it is also true of 'Music', 'Drama' and 'Art'. Once you try to apply a specific definition, you find that there are examples of non-literary phenomena to which it applies and literary phenomena to which it does not. Most literature is, of course, fiction but most people would also agree that not all fiction (eg comic books, nursery rhymes, and pornography) is literary. On the other hand travel journals (presumably non-fiction) are considered by many to be literature.

To read literature is therefore to become involved in a conspiracy. A publisher conspires with a writer to publish something the latter has written. The writer swears that he has written the book himself and not stolen the material from another writer (or indeed from police records, if it is our imagined short story). The publisher publishes the work in a series of books identified in a catalogue as literature. Then a critic reads the book and joins the conspiracy by accepting that it is indeed literature. He or she writes a review of it, identifying it as 'good' or 'bad' literature, according to personal experience and values. If he is a good critic, he or she considers qualities of style, structure, use of language, psychological insight, reflection of social issues, plotting and the like. A reader of this review is then prompted to buy the book and finds it shelved under 'Literature' or 'Fiction' in a local bookshop. The blurb confirms the fact that it is a novel. The reader then reads the work, bringing to bear on it ways of thinking learned through education to be appropriate to the reading of a novel. If the work is found to be 'good', it is recommended to a friend. Thus all parties have conspired to confirm the existence of a work of literature.

It was the realisation that what counted as 'literature' and 'good literature' in any given society at any given time was a matter of convention that enabled theorists to consider further how such conventions were established and the possibilities of alternative conventions. It made it possible to consider literature in close comparison with other cultural phenomena and in the light of theories developed to explain them.

Hazard Warnings

With literary interpretation, if anything goes, then nothing comes of it. The more it seems like madness, the more need there is to have method in it. The philosopher Karl Popper coined the very useful concept of 'falsifiability' to refer to a characteristic any theory must have if it is to be considered truly scientific. This concept enables one to identify many fields of study, in addition to those of the natural sciences, as incorporating rigorous criteria for the truth value of their findings. Basically, to be truly scientific, a theory must be 'falsifiable.' That is to say that it must be so formulated that it must be possible to predict under what circumstances it could be proven false. Of course, the flip-side of this is that it must also be possible to present evidence to demonstrate that it is true. A clear example of a pseudo-science, in other words a pseudo-theory, is astrology. It is obviously not possible to prove or disprove the influence of heavenly bodies on the fates of human beings. The fact that astrology is not falsifiable, of course, only encourages many to believe in it! What many do not realise, or will not admit, is that the concept of 'falsifiability' can also be applied to interpretations of literature and theories about literature.

Analysing a work of literature from whatever theoretical perspective also requires rigorous attention to evidence. If, leaving aside the vexed question of whether it is literature or not, one considers possible interpretations of the nursery rhyme about Miss Muffet who memorably sat on a tuffet eating her curds and whey, and who was promptly frightened away by a big spider, then it is possible, in principle, to prove or disprove, by rigorous historical research, the theory that the rhyme reflects the eating habits of poor country people. But it would be considerably more difficult to prove, or disprove, the validity of an interpretation which suggested that the spider symbolised a fear, common among country-girls at some time in the English Middle Ages, of being raped by dark strangers.

In my accounts of each of the theories explained in this book, I shall endeavour to indicate any problems in their application to literature. The sequence is not strictly chronological, although it is partly so. Theories dependent conceptually and logically on earlier ones do appear later in the book (post-structuralism after structuralism, feminism after psychoanalysis etc). As a final warning I would like to remind the reader that the interpretation of literature according to a specific theory can itself be reinterpreted according to another theory ad infinitum. In the words of Professor Morris Zapp in David Lodge's novel *Small World*, which satirises literary scholars, 'Every decoding is another encoding.'

A note on conventions in the text

When a quotation is identified by the author's name followed by a date and both are enclosed in brackets, this refers to the edition of the author's work included in the bibliography. Where the names of theorists and critics have been used as headings, their dates have been given when possible. When it has not proved possible to trace dates with certainty, they have been omitted.

The Literary Canon and New Criticism

Most books on the development of literary theory in England start with Matthew Arnold, because he ushered in an era in which literature was to be considered by influential critics as the central repository of English culture and values. These critics were to have lasting effects on the ways in which many generations of students perceived the significance of literature. F R Leavis and the poet T S Eliot, above all, established the notion of the existence of a literary canon of undeniably great works of literature. I A Richards, with his focus on close textual analysis, inspired the development of the so-called New Criticism in America.

Matthew Arnold (1822–1888)

Arnold, an educator, poet and professor of poetry at Oxford University, was of the opinion that literature, apart from its pleasing aesthetic qualities, had an educational role in people's lives. He believed that the persistence of English culture was threatened by the growth of Philistine values, which were being encouraged by the rise of a middle class obsessed with material wealth. As he believed that religion had been undermined by Darwin's theory of evolution, he

DAVID CARTER

expressed the wish that poetry would take its place in men's hearts. Poetry would interpret life for us all and console us, as indeed it had always done, dating back to antiquity. Arnold famously defined culture as 'the best that has been thought and said in the world' (*Culture and Anarchy*, 1869). This culture was to be a bulwark against the chaotic life of the working class and the illusions by which middle-class Protestants lived. Through culture it was possible to be free from fanaticism and move towards an existence of sweetness and light. Culture encouraged 'the growth and predominance of our humanity proper, as distinguished from our animality' (ibid).

The problem with Arnold's ideas for more recent theorists has been that he thought the values of the culture, which he espoused, were eternally true for every age and all conditions of human beings. All people, at all times, were capable of aspiring to the same ideals. The essence of true culture transcended history. Recent critics have found it difficult to go along with his notion of poets as somehow having access to eternally valid wisdom which they impart to others. Basically, Arnold saw literature as the domain of high-minded intellectuals and his definition excluded the writing of a large part of the populace.

T S Eliot (1888–1965)

After the First World War, the American-born poet, T S Eliot, took up Arnold's challenge and began to reassess the literary culture of England. In the words of the British theorist Terry Eagleton, he set about conducting 'a whole-sale salvage and demolition job on its literary traditions'

22

(Eagleton, 1983). Eliot was very largely responsible i formulating what already existed as a loosely drawn up list: the canon of English literature (the indisputably good and great works). He made poetry central to his theory and focused specifically on the poem as a text. For him poetry should be impersonal. In *Traditional and the Individual Talent* (1919), he asserted that a poet did not have 'a personality' to express but a particular medium. Poetry was to serve as an escape from the self: 'Poetry is not a turning loose of emotion, but an escape from emotion; it is not the expression of personality, but an escape from personality' (ibid). The poet's personal and social circumstances were secondary to the poetry itself, and he/she should not indulge in expressions of profound emotion, but seek what he called, in the essay *Hamlet* (1919), an 'objective correlative': 'a set of objects, a situation, a chain of events which shall be the formula of that particular emotion.' Emotion should be conveyed indirectly. Through the awareness of an ironic perception of the world and of paradoxes, the reader should be challenged and made to think. This meant of course that Eliot's canon of good poetry was severely limited in scope: he found little use for most of the poets in the previous two centuries!

Eliot considered literature (and especially poetry) to be in direct opposition to the modern world. Poetry could provide the profound experience that the modern world, with its utilitarian materialism, could not offer. Poetry especially could recapture a lost ideal of wholeness and convey complex meanings which we would otherwise simply not perceive. Eliot's ideas greatly influenced a group of academics at Cambridge University, including IA Richards and F R Leavis, who, in turn, were to exert long-lasting influence on critical thinking about literature.

The Newbolt Report

The importance of government education policy on the study of literature in schools should not be ignored. A government report entitled *The Teaching of English in England* (1921), the author of which was Sir Henry Newbolt, strongly encouraged the study of English literature in educational institutions. It is full of sentiment which owes much to Arnold and Eliot: 'Literature is not just a subject for academic study, but one of the chief temples of the Human Spirit, in which all should worship' and it is 'an embodiment of the best thoughts of the best minds, the most direct and lasting communication of experience by man to man.' For Newbolt, literature also had the function of creating a sense of national identity, serving to 'form a new element of national unity, linking together the mental life of all classes'. All these ideas, of course, were articulated in the aftermath of the First World War and have to be viewed in that context.

I A Richards (1893–1979)

Following Eliot's emphasis on the poem as text, Richards, an academic at Cambridge, with a background in aesthetics, psychology and semantics, published a widely influential book in 1924, *Principles of Literary Criticism*. He argued that criticism should emulate the precision of science and differentiate the 'emotive' language of poetry from the 'referential' language of non-literary works. For Richards, poets are able to articulate the chaos of the world around them and gain control of it. They can reconcile contradictions and transcend self-centredness. Literature helps us to evaluate our personal experiences. It conveys a certain type of knowledge which is not factual or scientific but concerned with values.

In his book *Practical Criticism* (1929), Richards included examples of work by his students, in which they attempted to analyse short unidentified poems. This exercise rapidly became the standard method of training students in critical analysis, both in Great Britain and America. As it involved the ruthless exclusion of any consideration of context, historical or social, and of the biography of the author, its scope was limited but it did have one positive effect. It nurtured the close reading of literary texts. Many subsequent theorists have lamented the passing of this skill. Richards left Cambridge in 1929 and settled at Harvard University. His subsequent work greatly influenced the development of what became known as American New Criticism.

William Empson (1906–1984)

William Empson was a student of Richards and he produced his first and most famous work, *Seven Types of Ambiguity* (1930), when he was still a student. For Empson, ambiguity was the defining characteristic of poetic language. He shared Richards' passion for close reading of texts, which has led many to ally him with the

American New Critics, but, in many ways, he was opposed to their major doctrines. He preferred to treat poetry as a type of utterance which has much continuity with ordinary ways of speech. He also took seriously into account what he conceived the author's intentions to be. He did not examine works in isolation but was concerned to consider how the words were used in social contexts. For him, a final coherent interpretation of a poem was impossible. The ambiguities he discovered in poetry could never be given a specific final interpretation. Poetic language was suggestive of inexhaustible meaning. For these reasons, his ideas have often found more sympathy with the common reader than with academic critics, concerned as they are, for the most part, with precise definition. Empson was a highly idiosyncratic thinker, not really belonging to any school, and is doubtless long overdue for reassessment.

New Criticism

American New Criticism, which was active from the late 1930s to the late 1950s, also took on most of the ideas of Eliot and Richards, as well as those of Empson. The movement had its roots in the American South, which had long been backward economically, but was then undergoing rapid modernisation. The leading critics had much sympathy with similar reactions against rapid modernisation among British critics. Prominent among the group were John Crowe Ransom, W K Wimsatt, Monroe C Beardsley, Cleanth Brooks and Mark Schorer.

For the New Critics, poetry was also central to their

concerns and seen as a quasi-religious defence against sterile scientific modes of thought. An alienated world could be reanimated. Poetry could remain untouched by the prevalent materialism all around. A poem existed as a self-evident, unique entity. It could not be paraphrased, nor could it be expressed other than as it was. Every element in a poem was in balanced integration with every other element, leading to a coherence of the whole. A poem was considered as an object in itself, cut off from both author and the world around it. This view was, of course, completely compatible with Richards' procedure of 'practical criticism'.

Yet New Criticism did not consider the poem to be cut off completely from reality. It was not, in other words, an entirely formalist approach, which would involve examining only the form of an isolated entity. The poem was seen somehow to incorporate the outside world within itself. In practice, New Criticism concentrated on paradoxes and ambivalence which could be established in the text.

For John Crowe Ransom, in an essay called *Criticism. Inc* (1937), a poem creates harmony and coherence from the chaos of experience: 'The poet perpetuates in his poem an order of existence which in actual life is constantly crumbling beneath his touch.' In *The Language of Paradox* (1942), Cleanth Brooks wrote that 'it wields together the discordant and the contradictory'.

W K Wimsatt and Monroe C Beardsley wrote two highly influential essays which advocated the importance of giving prime attention to the text. They isolated two common fallacies in literary interpretation. In *The*

DAVID CARTER

Intentional Fallacy (1946) they criticised the tendency to confuse what the author intended in the writing of a work of literature with what is actually there on the page. One should not speculate on what the writer may have wanted to say. In *The Affective Fallacy* (1949), they criticised readers who confuse their own emotional response to a work with what the poem itself really tells them. The way a work affects readers can too easily blur their vision. These views found echoes later in poststructuralist theory, though the latter has a different concept of the nature of a text.

New Criticism clearly focused predominantly on poetry but one writer, Mark Schorer, extended its main precepts to include analysis of prose fiction. In an essay entitled *Fiction and the Analogical Matrix* (1949), he concerns himself with the revelation of unconscious patterns of images and symbols which are present in all forms of fiction and which clearly go beyond authorial intentions. Meaning often contradicts surface sense but, while this theory may seem to prefigure deconstructive approaches, in reality Schorer emphasises the fact that prose fiction always ultimately manages to integrate all apparent contradictions into a coherent whole.

The Chicago School

New Criticism also spawned a group of critics with similar but fundamentally heretical views. They were known as 'The Chicago School' or the 'New Aristotelians', and were active from the late 1930s through the 1940s and 1950s. The central figure was R S Crane at the

University of Chicago. They derived their ideas basically from Aristotle and reacted against the principles of New Criticism, with its prime concern for poetry and its rejection of historical analysis. They believed in applying whatever method of analysis seemed appropriate to a particular case and were most influential in the study of narrative structure in the novel. Wayne C Booth, a later critic, in his book *The Rhetoric of Fiction* (1961), acknowledged his debt to the 'New Aristotelians.' He examined the methods, or rhetorical devices, employed by the author to communicate with readers, making an important distinction between the actual author and the 'authorial voice' in the work. He distinguished between 'reliable' and 'unreliable' narrators and promoted the view that authors do, indeed, intend to impose their values on the reader through the presence of a 'reliable' narrator.

F R Leavis (1895–1978) and D H Lawrence (1885–1930)

Leavis was instrumental in putting English and the study of English Literature at the heart of school and university curricula in England. However one may view his critical legacy, the study of the humanities in England owes much to his efforts. Especially important were his essays published as *Education and the University* (1943). He was very much concerned with the practical business of criticism and not with theorising about it, and regarded criticism and philosophy as completely separate activities. He adopted Richards' methods of practical criticism as well as the emphasis on the text stipulated by the New Critics.

For Leavis, a text should contain within it the full justification of why it is as it is and not otherwise. The first stage in the process of analysis was close scrutiny of the text (he gave the name *Scrutiny* to the journal he founded and edited from 1932 to 1953). Such close scrutiny led ultimately to establishing the 'Life' (a term never defined) of the text, its closeness to experience and its moral force.

In *Revaluation* (1936), Leavis delineated the 'true' English poetic tradition along the lines prescribed by Eliot, and in *The Great Tradition* (1948) he established the Leavisite (the word has entered common critical parlance) canon of great English novels. His great novelists (Jane Austen, George Eliot, Henry James, Joseph Conrad and Leavis' near contemporary D H Lawrence) promote, according to Leavis, full human awareness in the face of materialism and technology. Unlike Richards and the New Critics, Leavis brought a social and political awareness to bear in his analyses.

D H Lawrence, whom Leavis greatly admired, echoed Leavis' sentiments. In his essay *Morality and the Novel* (1925) he wrote: 'If a novel reveals true and vivid relationships, it is a moral work, no matter what the relationships may consist in.' And in *Why the Novel Matters* (1936) his concept of 'Life' is as mystically and vaguely defined as that of Leavis: 'To be alive, to be man alive, to be whole man alive: that is the point. And at its best, the novel, and the novel supremely, can help you.'

Many have regarded Leavis and the ideology of *Scrutiny* as essentially elitist: your soul is only really safe if you studied literature under Leavis, or at least under a Leavisite!

Russian Formalism

Both American and Russian Formalists were concerned to examine what was specifically literary about a text. As has been noted in the Introduction to the present volume, defining 'literariness' has proved to be virtually impossible, both because its attributes are not unique and because statements which are true about all literary works are not, on the whole, very useful. Early Formalism developed quite independently in America and Russia but it was Russian Formalism, which flourished during the pre- and post-revolutionary period in Russia, that had the more far-reaching effects.

As the name suggests, formalism, and especially Russian Formalism, was more interested in analysis of form, the structure of a text and its use of language, than in content. Formalists wanted to establish a scientific basis for the study of literature. The credo of the early Russian Formalists was an extreme one: they believed that the human emotions and ideas expressed in a work of literature were of secondary concern and provided the context only for the implementation of literary devices. Unlike the New Criticism in America, they were not interested in the cultural and moral significance of literature, but wished to explore how various literary devices produced certain aesthetic effects.

The Three Phases

It has been argued that there are three distinct phases in the development of Russian Formalism which can be characterised by three metaphors. The first phase regarded literature as a kind of machine with various devices and functioning parts; the second phase considered it to be more like an 'organism'; and the third phase saw literary texts as 'systems.' Particularly influential in the early phase of Russian Formalism was Viktor Shklovsky.

Viktor Shklovsky (1893–1984)

Shklovsky was the leading light in a group of literary critics based in St Petersburg and known as 'Opayaz'. They encouraged experimental literature and art. Shklovsky's essay *Art as Technique*, published in 1917, served as a manifesto for the group. In this essay several concepts were formulated which are crucial to understanding the philosophical premises of Russian Formalism. The first of these is 'habitualisation.' This refers to the fact that, as we become familiar with things, we no longer really perceive them: '…as perception becomes habitual, it becomes automatic.' Related to this idea is what Shklovsky called the 'algebraic' method of thought. Through 'habitualisation' we come to think of things in only the most general way and conceive of them only in ways akin to algebraic symbols. Thus a chair loses its individuality and becomes just the thing we sit on. We no longer perceive its texture, its sheen, its precise design etc. This leads to Shklovsky's third and probably most famous concept, that of 'defamiliarisation' (*ostranenie* which means literally 'making strange'). This he considers the main function of art: 'And art exists that one may recover the sensation of life; it exists to make one feel things, to make the stone *stony*. The purpose of art is to impart the sensation of things as they are perceived and not as they are known.' He then proceeds to demonstrate how some great writers (Tolstoy and Pushkin) have consciously used the technique of 'defamiliarisation.' It is also in this essay that we find the famous formulation which makes clear the priorities of Russian Formalist aesthetics: 'the object is not important.'

Theories of Narrative

Theories of narrative featured prominently in Russian Formalist thought, especially distinctions between 'story' and 'plot.' This was not, of course, new in the theory of literature. The distinction goes back at least to Aristotle, for whom plot (*mythos*) or 'the arrangement of the incidents' was clearly different to the story on which it was based. The time sequence of events in a Greek tragedy, for example, is clearly different to that of the events it relates. Usually the tragedy starts with a report of what happened before and then the audience is plunged into the middle of events (*in medias res*), with occasional references back to earlier stages in the story.

Boris Tomashevski developed further a concept that Shklovsky had first formulated in his essay on the English author Lawrence Sterne's *Tristram Shandy*. The basic material of the story was termed *fabula*. Tomashevski contrasted this with *suzhet*, the story as it is actually told. One *fabula* can provide material for many *suzhet*, a notion which was taken up by later formalists and was also to provide a link with structuralism. These formalist distinctions are not essentially a reformulation of Aristotelian concepts because the Russian Formalists conceived the effects and purposes of *suzhet* differently to those of Aristotle's *mythos*. For Aristotle, plot had to be plausible, have a degree of inevitability and provide insight into the human condition. For the Russian Formalists, on the other hand, the function of plot was to defamiliarise what we are observing, to make us aware of the artificiality of the process of literary creation.

The Russian Formalists also had an idiosyncratic notion of 'motivation', using the concept not with the meaning of 'intention, or purpose', but in relation to the structural concept of a 'motif'. Tomashevski was the one to elucidate the distinction. It is a unit of construction: the smallest unit of a plot, a single statement, or action, for example. Tomashevski distinguished between 'bound' and 'free' motifs. A 'bound' motif is necessitated by the original story (for example, the pact with Mephistopheles in Goethe's *Faust*) but a 'free' motif is not necessary in the same way. It is part of the artifice of the work (for example, Goethe's decision to set the scene with a 'Prologue in Heaven' at the beginning of his play). The term 'motif' came about because the Russian Formalists perceived the ideas and themes of a work as secondary, as motivations (in the more usual sense) for the literary devices. They argued that a constant awareness of the distinction between 'bound' and 'free' motifs is necessary because, when an unfamiliar device or 'free' motif is included, it serves for a while to make us aware of the artificiality of the text but eventually it too becomes familiar or conventional. For example, when playing with the time sequence became the norm, both in literature and in the cinema, then that device could no longer have a defamiliarising effect.

Jan Mukařovský

Jan Mukařovský is usually categorised among the structuralists but his roots are in Russian Formalist thought and he is certainly a significant transitional figure. He was a member of the Prague Linguistic Circle, founded in 1926. He developed Shklovsky's concept of 'defamiliarisation' more systematically, using the term 'foregrounding' instead. He defines this as 'the aesthetically intentional distortion of the literary components'. For Mukařovský, 'foregrounding' has the effect of 'automatizing' other aspects of the text in close proximity to it. That is to say, it makes us no longer sensitive to them. The other objects have become, to use Shklovsky's terminology again, over-familiar to us. The term 'foregrounding' clearly comes from the visual arts (painting and photography providing the clearest examples). Through focusing (by means of perspective or adjustment of lens) upon figures or events in the front ('foreground') of a picture, the 'background' is not subjected to our conscious attention. 'Defamiliarisation' makes what is familiar appear strange only but 'foregrounding' reveals the whole work to be a complicated and interrelated structure. It is not surprising, there-fore, that the concept was taken up by more explicitly structuralist theorists. It can be compared to the notion of the 'dominant' developed by Roman Jakobson.

Mukařovský, unlike earlier Russian Formalists, did not consider the object, of which a literary work was a treat-ment, to be of secondary interest. Indeed, he emphasised the dynamic tension between literature and society in the creation of literature. He argued also that an object can have several functions. Often the aesthetic function is just one of many. A simple and obvious example is that a church can be both a place of worship and a work of art. A speech can be political or legal rhetoric and also a work of art. (Arguably, this is the case with many of Winston Churchill's and certainly it is so with several in Shakespeare's *Julius Caesar*.) What is considered to be art changes in close rela-tion to the tastes and preferences of a given society. In *Aesthetic Function, Norm and Value as Social Facts* (1936), Mukařovský argued that aesthetic function cannot exist in isolation from its place and time, nor without considering the person evaluating it. He distinguished between the 'material object', the actual book or other physical object, and the 'aesthetic object', which can exist only in the mind of the person who interprets the 'material object'.

The Bakhtin School

The attribution of several important works to Mikhail Bakhtin is disputed. Three theorists worked closely together and precise attribution may never be obtained. The three associates were Mikhail Bakhtin, Pavel

Medvedev and Valentin Volosinov. As a student and teacher in the 1920s, Bakhtin began to take a critical stance against Russian Formalism but the ideas of the three may be considered formalist in their interest in the linguistic structure of literary works. Also, the three men believed in the social nature of language and reveal clear influence of Marxist thought. But they differed from orthodox Marxists in their assumptions about the relationship between language and ideology. For them, ideology is not a reflex of socio-economic conditions but is conditioned by the medium through which it manifests itself: language. And language is a material reality. The meanings of words change according to the different social and historical situations in which they are used. Multiple meanings are in fact the normal condition of language ('heteroglossia'). The reflection of social interaction (in the novel, for instance) reveals this 'heteroglossia'. The novel which embodies a single authorial voice is, in fact, a distortion of natural language, imposing unity of vision where naturally there is none. The monologue has always been an unnatural genre.

Bakhtin, in particular, developed these ideas in relation to literary texts, principally in three works: *Problems of Dostoievsky's Art*, the revised version *Problems in Dostoevsky's Poetics* (1963) and *Rabelais and his World* (1966). He argued that all language partakes of the nature of dialogue. Every speech is inspired by a previous utterance and expects a future response. And the language always seems to encourage reflection on its own nature. In this respect, Bakhtin is still essentially a formalist. In *From the Prehistory of Novelistic Discourse* (probably written in

1940 but first published in Russia in 1967) he wrote: 'To a greater or lesser extent, every novel is a dialogized system made up of the images of "languages", styles and consciousnesses that are concrete but inseparable from language. Language in the novel not only represents, but itself serves as the object of representation. Novelistic discourse is always criticizing itself.'

Roman Jakobson (1896–1982)

Roman Jakobson was a bridge between Russian Formalism and Structuralism. He was a founder member of the Moscow Linguistic Circle and all his writings reveal the centrality of linguistic theory in his thought and especially the influence of Saussure (see chapter 3). He was also an enthusiastic supporter of experimental poets. In 1920, he moved to Czechoslovakia and helped to found the influential Prague Linguistic Circle. With the Nazi invasion of Czechoslovakia in 1939, he left the country and finally settled in the USA in 1941.

Apart from his linguistic research Jakobson gained respect for his very precise linguistic analyses of classic works of literature. He and Claude Lévi-Strauss, the French anthropologist, were also colleagues at the New School of Social Research in New York from 1941. They collaborated on an analysis of Baudelaire's poem *Les Chats*, which not only became famous as a typical structuralist analysis but also drew much negative criticism. Jakobson attempted the daunting task of trying to define 'literariness' in linguistic terms. His paper *Linguistics and Poetics*, delivered at a conference in 1958 and published as

Style in Language in 1960, provides the clearest expression of his ideas on the topic. Even when we transpose a work of literature, he argues, from one medium to another (eg a novel into a film, an epic into a comic book) certain structural features are preserved, 'despite the disappearance of their verbal shape'. Many features of a work are not limited to the language in which it is expressed. The 'truth value' of a work, for example, or its significance as a myth are obviously 'extralinguistic entities'. Such aspects 'exceed the bounds of poetics and of linguistics in general'.

It would seem that Jakobson is here going beyond a purely formalist approach but, while revealing his awareness of such dimensions, he is firm in restricting himself to the purely linguistic: '...no manifesto, foisting a critic's own tastes and opinions on creative literature, may act as substitute for an objective scholarly analysis of verbal art.' Another idea of his which proved to be especially relevant to modern literary theory was the postulation of two fundamental poles of organising discourse that can be traced in every kind of cultural product: metaphor and metonymy. This idea was developed as a result of investigating the mental disorder of aphasia (expounded at length in *Fundamentals of Language*, 1956, which he published together with Morris Halle). In the sentence 'The ship crossed the sea', the sentence can be made metaphorical by selecting a different verb, for example by comparing the motion of the ship to that of a plough ('The ship ploughed the sea'). Metonymy is the use of an attribute of something to suggest the whole thing. For example, deepness can suggest the sea ('The ship crossed the deep'). Metaphor depends on the combination of things not necessarily associated or contiguous, whereas metonymy utilises closely associated attributes.

This led Jakobson to make some interesting characterisations of different literary schools according to their positions on the metaphor-metonymy axis: 'The primacy of the metaphoric process in the literary schools of romanticism and symbolism has been repeatedly acknowledged, but it is still insufficiently realized that it is the predominance of metonymy which underlies and actually predetermines the so-called "realistic" trend, which belongs to an intermediary stage between the decline of romanticism and the rise of symbolism and is opposed to both.'

Jakobson developed the concepts of 'defamiliarisation' and 'foregrounding' further to characterise whole schools of critical and literary thought. In the dynamic system of a work of literature elements are structured in relation to each other as foreground and background. A foregrounded element was referred to by the later Russian Formalists as 'the dominant.' Jakobson regarded 'the dominant' as one of the most important late formalist concepts. He defined it as 'the focusing component of a work of art; it rules, determines and transforms the remaining components'. Literary forms change and develop as a result of a 'shifting dominant'. He believed that the literary theory (or poetics) of a particular period might be governed by a 'dominant' which derives from a non-literary system. For example, the theory of Renaissance poetry was derived from the visual arts and that of Realism from verbal art. The basic elements of the system do not change (plot, diction, syntax etc) but the functions of the elements do.

Structuralism

Structuralism challenged many of the most cherished beliefs of both critics and readers: the assumption that a literary work expresses an author's mind and personality and that it also tells some essential truth about human life. Structuralists state bluntly that the author is dead and that literary discourse has no truth function. In an essay of 1968, the French theorist Roland Barthes put the structuralist view in perhaps its most forceful form. He claimed that writers only have the power to mix already existing writings, to reassemble them. They cannot use writing to express themselves but can only draw on language, which is already formulated, and culture, which is essentially already expressed in language (in Barthes' words it is 'always already written'). Structuralists also describe themselves as anti-humanist because they oppose all forms of literary criticism in which the meaning is related to a human subject. Of course, if all these tenets were demonstrably true, then writers might as well cast aside their pens and reach for their knitting needles.

Ferdinand de Saussure (1857–1913)

Concepts formulated by one man have greatly influenced

the whole of modern literary theory. He is included here among the structuralists because that is where his influence is particularly strong but the whole of cultural theory is permeated by distinctions first drawn up by him. If there is some truth in the claim that the whole of western philosophy is but a series of footnotes to Plato, then the same could be said of the relationship between cultural (hence also literary) theory and Ferdinand de Saussure.

Important for structuralist theory is his distinction between 'langue' and 'parole'. 'Langue' is the language system which we all share and which we unconsciously draw on when we speak; 'parole' is language as we actually realize it in individual utterances. For Saussure, the proper study for linguistics is the underlying system and not the individual utterances. Structuralist literary critics also endeavoured to study the underlying rules, or grammar, of a work and not its idiosyncrasies.

Another famous distinction made by Saussure is that between 'signifier' and 'signified'. For him, words do not refer directly to things. There is, in other words, no discernible connection between a word and the thing to which it refers. Words are signs with two aspects: the 'signifier' and the 'signified'. What is written or spoken is the 'signifier' and what is thought when the word is written or uttered is the 'signified'. Meaning is perceived not through the word's relation to something but in understanding it as part of a system of relationships, as part of a sign-system. This mode of analysis can be applied not only to language but to a whole range of phenomena. The most common and easily comprehensible illustration of the principle is in the system of traffic lights. Red, amber and green have no intrinsic meanings but mean 'stop', 'get ready' and 'go' only in relation to each other in the context of a set of traffic lights. The science of such sign systems is called semiotics or semiology, which are related to structuralism, but structuralism also concerns itself with systems, such as kinship relations, which do not utilise signs. In this respect, structuralism reveals that it has important roots in the anthropology of Claude Lévi-Strauss. The basic importance of structuralism for a study of literature derives from its interest in underlying structures of sign systems. The assumption is that such structures are even more basic than form, more basic therefore than conventional notions of literary form. Structures are considered as somehow enabling meaning to emerge.

Semiotics

The term 'semiotics' (or the alternative term 'semiology') is frequently used in close association with the theory of structuralism. In the previous section, it was referred to as a science of signs. It has been argued that literary structuralists are really engaging in semiotics, so some distinctions should be made clear. Structuralism is, strictly speaking, a method of investigation, whereas semiotics can be described as a field of study. Its field is that of sign systems.

I. C S Peirce (1839–1914)

The American philosopher C S Peirce drew up three useful distinctions between different types of sign (in Saussure's sense of the word).

1. The 'Iconic' is a sign which resembles its referent (eg on road signs a picture of a ship near a port, or a car falling off a quayside). The word 'icon' is of course still used for images representing the Virgin Mary in the Russian Orthodox Church. Nowadays the word is most commonly used to refer to those little images identifying various functions on a computer.
2. The 'Indexical' is a sign associated, sometimes causally, with a referent (eg smoke as a sign indicating fire, or a flash as a warning about electricity).
3. The 'Symbolic' is a sign which has only an arbitrary relation to its referent, as is the case with words in a language.

These terms were generally adopted by semioticians and further classifications were developed. What a sign stands for is called 'denotation' and what other signs are associated with it is 'connotation'. There are also 'paradigmatic' signs, which may replace each other in the system, and 'syntagmatic' signs, which are linked together in a chain. A sign system which refers to another sign system is called a 'metalanguage' (literary theory itself is a good example of this). And signs which have more than one meaning are called 'polysemic'. With this short list the range of terminology is not exhausted.

II. Yury Lotman

The Russian semiotician Yury Lotman did much to develop the application of the theory of semiotics to literature, most famously in *The Analysis of the Poetic Text*

(1976). He was very much concerned not to restrict himself to pure structural analysis but also to introduce a degree of evaluation of the text. He combined strict structural analysis with close reading of the text in the mode of New Criticism and argued that literary texts were more worthy of our attention than non-literary ones because they carried a 'higher information load'. He describes a poem, for example, as being 'semantically saturated'. A poor poem for him carries insufficient information. A poem consists of a complex arrangement of interrelated systems (phonological, metrical, lexical etc) and poetic effects are created through tensions between these systems. There is a norm, or standard, for each system, from which the poet can deviate, or which can clash with the norms of another system. Sentence structure, for example, may not correspond with the standard metric pattern. The reader becomes more aware of relations of meaning between words when they are placed in some unusual metric or other structural relationships to each other. In this way, the reader can perceive new significances beyond dictionary definitions. Lotman argues that a poem can in effect only be re-read. To read it once is not to read it at all because some of its effects can only be perceived with a knowledge of the structural complexity. What we perceive in a poetic text is only the result of awareness of contrasts and differences. Even the absence of an expected effect can produce meaning, such as when the reader is led to expect a rhyme which does not appear. Lotman did not believe however that poetry and literature could be adequately defined by linguistic analysis alone. The text had to be seen in wider relation to other systems of meaning, not only within the literary tradition but in society generally.

Phoneme Theory

It may not be immediately obvious how phoneme theory could be of relevance to literary theory but the French critic Roland Barthes made it central to his analysis of the short story *Sarrasine* by the author Balzac. A phoneme is a distinct unit of sound in a language which distinguishes one word from another, for example the *p*, *b*, *d* and *t* in the English words *pad*, *pat*, *bad* and *bat*. A word can be pronounced in a variety of ways, with different stresses and accents etc, and the whole word will remain distinguishable and therefore recognizable as long as the individual phonemes remain recognizable. There is of course no ideal phoneme but only a mental abstraction of it. All actually occurring sounds are variations of phonemes. The logical consequence of this is that we do not recognize sounds in their own right but only by distinguishing them from others.

The relevance of this theory for cultural and literary analysis is that it presupposes an underlying system, or structure, of paired opposites at the very basic level of language. In phoneme theory, it manifests itself in pairs which are, for example, nasalised/non-nasalised, voiced/unvoiced etc. Such 'binary oppositions' occur in many cultural phenomena and have been especially fruitful in anthropological analyses by, for example, Mary Douglas and Claude Lévi-Strauss who analysed rites and kinship structures by adapting phoneme theory to examine the underlying system of differences between practices. Roland Barthes adapted the procedure to analyse all kinds of human activities, from clothes to cuisine. His early essays, collected in *Mythologies* (1957) and *Système de la mode* (1967), are accessible and enjoyable books. His ideas will be considered again later in the context of Post-structuralism.

Structuralist Narratology

Structuralist narrative theory uses the model of linguistic analysis to reveal the structure of narrative. The basis model for that of a storyline is that of grammatical syntax. Narrative is compared to the structure of a sentence. Especially influential on the development of structuralist narratology was Vladimir Propp.

I. Vladimir Propp (1895–1970)

Tomashevski's distinctions between *fabula* and *suzhet* were taken up by Vladimir Propp and applied to the analysis of fairy tales. Propp was not a formalist and used the terms for purely structural analysis. He realised that if you look closely at traditional Russian fairy tales and folk tales, you find one basic story structure underlying them all: many *suzhets* derived from one basic *fabula*. There might be superficial differences between the stories, in terms of the individual details of events and characters, but all can be reduced to the same basic structure. To demonstrate this Propp devised the categories of 'actors' and 'functions'. 'Actors' are the types of central characters who appear and 'functions' are the acts or events which carry the narrative forward. There is a limited number of 'actors', the main ones being the following: the hero, the villain, the seeker (often identical with the hero), the helper, the false helper and the princess. And there are thirty-one functions which always appear in the same sequence, although not all of them appear in every story. Some common ones are: the setting of a task or challenge, successful completion of the task or overcoming the challenge, recognition of the hero, exposure of the villain, marriage of the hero etc. It is therefore possible to fit virtually all popular fairy tales into this basic pattern. The comparison with sentence structure is, in the first instance, a very simple one. The 'actors' are the subject of the sentences and the 'functions' are the predicates. It is clear also that many of Propp's 'actors' and 'functions' are to be found in all kinds of literary narratives and are most clearly defined in myths, epics and romances. Needless to say the reader is not usually aware of this underlying structure, nor is it necessary to be. The recognition that this kind of structural analysis was possible for all fairy tales inspired the hope of pursuing such analysis of literature in general.

II. A J Greimas (1917–1992)

A J Greimas (*Sémantique Structurale*, 1966) developed and expanded Propp's theory to make it applicable to various genres. His approach was based on a semantic analysis of sentence structure. He proposed three pairs of binary oppositions which include all six main 'actors' (*actants*) necessary: Subject/Object, Sender/Receiver, Helper/Opponent. He thereby made Propp's scheme more abstract, stressing neither a narrative form nor a specific type of character but a structural unit. These six *actants* can be combined into three structural units which he believed recur in all kinds of narrative:

1. Subject/Object: desire, search or aim.
2. Sender/Receiver: communication.
3. Helper/Opponent: auxiliary support or hindrance.

The most basic structure is the first. The subject is the main element, though not necessarily a person, in a story. This subject desires to achieve a certain object through its (his, her) action. It is this desire which moves the narrative along. The pattern as applied to actual texts becomes more complex than this, with various permutations.

Greimas also reduced Propp's thirty-one functions to twenty and grouped them into three 'syntagms' (structures): 'contractual', 'performative', and 'disjunctive'. The first of these is perhaps the most common. As its name suggests the 'contractual syntagm' involves the setting up or breaking of contracts, rules or systems of order. Thus, a narrative may adopt either of two structures: there is a contract or other principle of order, which is violated and subsequently punished, or there is the absence of such a contract (disorder) with a subsequent establishment of order. Greek tragedies and some of Shakespeare's plays conform to the first structure and American novels of the Wild West conform to the second. It must be stressed that Greimas' approach enables the reader to identify how meaning is created in the text but does not imply any specific interpretation. This the reader must supply for him- or herself.

III. Tzvetan Todorov (1939–)

Tzvetan Todorov took the ideas of both Propp and Greimas to what one might term their logical conclusion. He describes narrative structure using common syntactic concepts: agency, predication, adjectival and verbal functions, mood, aspect, etc. The basic unit of narrative is the proposition, which can either be an agent (such as a person) or a predicate (such as action). A predicate can also function like an adjective, describing the state of something, or it can function like a verb, indicating some kind of action. There are two higher levels of organisation above that of proposition: the sequence and the text. The basic sequence is made up of five propositions describing a state, which is subsequently disturbed and then re-established, though usually in a different form. The five propositions in sequence are: equilibrium (1), force (1), disequilibrium, force (2) and equilibrium (2). A succession of such sequences forms a text. Various complexities and permutations of the sequences can, of course, be introduced, connecting them in different ways, embedding one within another, digressing and returning etc. A work of literature is thus read as though it were one extended and complex sentence. Such a theory provides an apparently scientific procedure but it contributes little, if anything, to an actual understanding of meaning.

One of Todorov's most well-known studies is *The Typology of Detective Fiction* (1966), in which he distinguishes three basic types of detective fiction, which have evolved over time: the 'whodunit', the 'thriller' and the 'suspense novel'. This study also confirms the view that it is much easier to apply structuralist techniques of analysis to popular fiction than to more 'literary' works.

IV. Gérard Genette (1930–)

Gérard Genette's *Narrative Discourse* (1972) is regarded by many as one of the most important contributions to narratology. He redefined existing categories and introduced a number of completely new ones. For example he redefined the Russian Formalist distinctions between *fabula* and *suzhet* by dividing narrative into three levels: 'story' (*histoire*), 'discourse' (*récit*) and narration. This is most clearly perceived in texts in which there is a distinct narrator or storyteller addressing the reader directly ('narration'). He or she presents a verbal 'discourse', in which he or she also appears as a character in the events related ('story'). These three levels are related to each other by three aspects, which Genette derived from the three common aspects of verbs: 'tense', 'mood' and 'voice'. While the aspect of 'tense' may be readily understood by its reference to situating the story and/or the 'narration' in present or past time, those of 'mood' and 'voice' need further clarification. Both are important in analysing the point of view in a text. 'Mood' here refers to the perspective from which events are viewed (eg from that of a particular character) which may actually be described by a different narrative 'voice' (it might for example be an old man telling of the events of his own youth). Genette formulated a distinction between two different kinds of relation between narrator and character in terms of a binary opposition: there is 'homodiegetic' narrative, in which the narrator tells us about him/herself, and there is 'heterodiegetic' narrative, in which the narrator tells us about third persons. A 'homodiegetic' narrator is always in some way involved in the world narrated. A 'heterodiegetic' narrator is never involved in that world. Genette also used the term 'focalisation', which has proved to be of lasting usefulness in literary theory for describing some of the more complex relations between narrator and the world narrated. This term is especially useful when dealing with uncertain or shifting perspectives. In the case, for example, of what is known as free indirect discourse (revealing the thoughts of characters in their own idiom, but in the third person and tense of the narration). Sometimes it becomes difficult to distinguish between the 'voice' of the narrator and that of the character. If the narration has yielded in this way to the perspective of the character but still maintains the third person form (eg 'He knew he would always love her'), then this narrative can be described as being related through a 'focaliser'.

Genette's theory is more complex than I have been able to outline here and he employed a wider range of technical vocabulary than can be defined in the present context but one more of its achievements needs to be highlighted. In the essay *Frontiers of Narrative* (1966), he explored and criticised three pairs of commonly maintained binary oppositions in a way which prefigures, to some extent, the approach of deconstructive theory. The first opposition is that which Aristotle formulated in his *Poetics* of 'diegesis' (the author speaking in his own voice) and 'mimesis' (representation of what someone else actually said). Genette argued that 'mimesis' in this sense is simply not possible, as part of a text can never be what someone actually said. It is also narrative. The second opposition is that between narration and description. Narration, telling about the actions and events in a story, would appear to be different in kind to describing things, people and circumstances. However, Genette demonstrated that the very choice of nouns and verbs in a sentence telling of an action is part of the description. He dissolved the distinction. 'The man closed his hand into a ball' can become descriptive of quite a different situation if one changes the verb and a few of the nouns: 'The stranger clenched his hand into a fist.' The third opposition is that between narrative (a pure telling of a story uninfluenced by the subjectivity of the author) and discourse (in which the reader is aware of the nature of the teller). Genette demonstrated that pure narrative with no trace of authorial perspective is very rare indeed and difficult to maintain.

Structuralist Poetics

Jonathan Culler took as his premise in *Structuralist Poetics* (1975) that linguistics provided the best model for the analysis of literature. He wanted to explore 'the conventions that enable readers to make sense of' works of literature, believing that it was impossible to establish rules that govern the actual writing of texts. Structure could be found underlying the reader's interpretation of a text. In a later work, *The Pursuit of Signs* (1981), he attempted to explain the fact that readers, while following the same interpretative conventions, often produce different interpretations of, for example, a poem. One reason for this is that readers expect to find unity in a work but they employ different models of unity and apply such models to the actual work in different ways. In this book, however, Culler did not consider the effects of the reader's own ideology on perceptions of meaning. Using Chomsky's notion of underlying 'competence', Culler argued that a poet or novelist writes on the assumption of such a 'competence' in the reader. Just as we need linguistic 'competence' to make sense of what we hear or read, so we make use of 'literary competence', acquired through experience and institutional education, to make sense of literature. In more recent works, especially in *Framing the Sign* (1988), Culler has questioned more the institutional and ideological basis of the concept of 'literary competence' and, in his popular introduction, *Literary Theory* (1997), he summed up structuralism as attempting to 'analyse structures that operate unconsciously (structures of language, of the psyche, of society)'. But he still emphasised that structuralist poetics is not essentially concerned with establishing meaning: 'it seeks not to produce new interpretations of works but to understand how they can have the meanings and effects that they do.'

Marxist Theory

The Essence of Marxist Thought

There is no scope in the present context to expound Marxist theory adequately. All that can be done is to stress the aspects of it, the essential concepts, which are relevant to understanding a Marxist approach to the study of literature. For Karl Marx, and those closest to his way of thinking, all those modes of thought, including literary creativity, are ideological and are products of social and economic existence. Basically Man's social being determines his consciousness and the material interests of the dominant social class determine how all classes perceive their existence. All forms of culture, therefore, do not exist in an ideal, abstract form but are inseparable from the historical determining social conditions. They exist, in other words, as a superstructure to the basic economic structure of a society. This view was the exact reverse of the Hegelian belief that the world was governed by thought and the application of reason, whether it be human or divine. Philosophising about the world alone was insufficient for Marx; the most important thing was to change it. In *The German Ideology* (1846), Marx and Friedrich Engels wrote of religion, morality and philosophy as 'phantoms found in the brains of men'. But in letters which he wrote in the 1890s Engels acknowledged that both he and Marx recognised that art, philosophy and other forms of human consciousness could alter the human condition and had a degree of autonomy. The special status of literature was also recognised by Marx in the *Grundrisse*. Greek tragedy was for him an anomaly because it seemed to represent a timeless, universal achievement but was actually produced within a society with a structure and ideology which he could no longer consider valid. How could such a phenomenon continue to give aesthetic pleasure and be regarded as expressing universal truths?

Socialist Realism

Socialist Realism is the term usually applied to the state-sanctioned theory of art favoured predominantly in the Soviet Union, and therefore known as Soviet Socialist Realism, but it was also the dominant party aesthetic in other Eastern European countries under the political domination of Russia after the Stalinist period and the Second World War. Basically the ideal of nineteenth century Russian realist literature was set up as the most suitable norm for a communist aesthetic but it was given a doctrinaire edge. All other forms of modernist experimental art and literature were considered to be the decadent offspring of late capitalism. Only lip service was paid to the notion of artistic freedom. In practise, a writer could not hope to get his work published if he or she did not write to please the party. Lenin had made this explicit in his essay *Party Organisation and Party Literature* (1905), in which he asserted that writers were free to write whatever they wanted but, if they wanted to get their work published in party journals, they would have to toe the party line. As all journals were soon to become affiliated to the party, this provided writers, effectively, with only Hobson's choice. Literary critics were encouraged to praise those writers of the past who had revealed insights into the social problems and developments of their time, even though they might have been of bourgeois origin themselves. Leo Tolstoy, Honoré de Balzac and Charles Dickens therefore came in for special praise. All literature had also to address the interests of the people as a whole. This quality was known as *narodnost*. And it had to present a progressive and, of course, communist outlook for the future of society.

Georg Lukács (1885–1971)

One of the most admired Marxist critics is Georg Lukács, a Hungarian-born philosopher and critic. He is associated with socialist realism but reveals great subtlety in his arguments. He greatly admired many of the great Realist works of the 19th century, especially when they revealed underlying contradictions in society. It was for this reason that he praised the novels of the Prussian writer Theodor Fontane, especially his short novel *Schach von Wuthenow* (translated as *A Man of Honour*), which provides a disturbing critique of the Prussian code of honour. For Lukács, it was 'the pinnacle of German historical narrative art'. In Lukács' eyes, true Realism did not just depict the appearance of the social world but provided 'a truer, more complete, more vivid and more dynamic reflection of reality'. A Realist novel does not provide an illusion of reality but is 'a special form of reflecting reality'. A truly realistic work provides a sense of the 'artistic necessity' of the scenes and details presented. The writer reflects, in an intensified form, the structure of the society depicted and its dialectical development. Lukács' ideas are expounded most fully in two major works: *The Historical Novel* (1937) and *Studies in European Realism* (1950). In *The Meaning of Contemporary Realism* (1957), he attacks especially modernist literature. He rejected the static, ahistorical epic structure of James Joyce's work, and found modernist writing, in general, lacking in historical awareness. Beckett and Kafka were condemned for these reasons. For Lukács, modernist writers were too concerned about evoking an inner stream of consciousness and the obsessions of isolated individuals. This he related to the effects of living in late capitalist societies. One of the few contemporaries he did admire was Thomas Mann, whom he considered an exponent of a genuine 'critical realism'. During a stay in Berlin in the 1930s he also attacked the use of modernist techniques in the writings of left-wing radicals. His attack on the playwright and theorist Bertolt Brecht has become particularly famous.

Bertolt Brecht (1898–1956)

After reading Marx in the 1920s, Bertolt Brecht, the German-born playwright, focused his earlier anarchistic attitudes into more clearly defined communist convictions. He wrote many clearly didactic plays (the *Lehrstücke)* and more complex thought-provoking plays, mainly in exile from Nazi Germany. His theoretical works on theatre practice revolutionised modern drama. He rejected entirely the Aristotelian tradition of theatre: plot, fate and universality were out. He employed techniques to bring about what he called a *Verfremdungseffekt*, meaning literally 'the effect of making strange' and usually translated as 'alienation'. It has much in common with the concept of 'defamiliarisation' coined by the Russian Formalists. By such methods he attempted to show up the contradictions in capitalist society as something strange and unnatural, requiring change. His actors were not to create the illusion of real people with whom audiences could identify but should present caricatures revealing the inner contradictions of the characters, the ways in which their behaviour was moulded by social forces and their need to survive.

One aspect of Brecht's theory, which brought him into conflict with Lukács, was the rejection of formal unity in a work. His 'epic' theatre consisted of a series of loosely-related episodes, rather than an all-embracing structure. The unities of time and place were rejected. He did not believe in any 'eternal aesthetic laws' and, for him, any dramatic device was acceptable if it served his purpose. He strongly opposed what he saw as Lukács' attempts to establish 'purely formal and literary criteria of realism'. He demanded constant adjustment to the ever-changing nature of political reality: 'to represent it the means of representation must alter too.'

The Frankfurt School

The name 'The Frankfurt School' has come to be applied to a group of philosophers and thinkers of other disciplines who were members or were associated with The Institute for Social Research in Frankfurt am Main in Germany. They practised what they called 'Critical Theory'. The leading figures in the group were Theodor Adorno, Max Horkheimer and Herbert Marcuse. The institute moved to New York during the Nazi period but settled back in Frankfurt again in 1950. Their analysis of modern culture and society was very much influenced by their experience of Fascism.

Theodor Adorno (1903–1969)

The leading and most influential writer on aesthetics in the Frankfurt School was undoubtedly Adorno. He criticised Lukács' view that art could have a direct relationship with reality. For Adorno, art, including literature, is detached from reality and this is the very source of its strength. Popular art forms only confirm and conform to the norms of a society but true art takes up a critical stance, distanced from the world which engendered it: 'Art is the negative knowledge of the actual world.' He saw the alienation evident in the writings of Proust and Beckett as proving such 'negative knowledge' of the modern world.

Walter Benjamin (1892–1940)

Walter Benjamin was closely associated with the Frankfurt School but he was very much a maverick thinker. His early writing was on Goethe and German Baroque drama. His best known essay is undoubtedly *The Work of Art in the Age of Mechanical Reproduction*, in which he argued that modern means of reproducing works of art, especially photography and film, have changed the special status of a work of art. This is also true, of course, of the reproduction of musical performances. Benjamin argues that works of art once used to have the quality of uniqueness which he calls their 'aura'. Even in the case of literature which, of course, had long been available in multiple copies, this aura had been maintained. Many kinds of modern works of art are actually designed with a view to reproducing them, as is the case with art prints, for example. In the case of the cinema there exist multiple copies without there being a real original from which the film is derived. Benjamin believed this to be a good and beneficial development, making art no longer something remote and awe-inspiring but accessible to intelligent lay analysis. One might argue against Benjamin, of course, that the result has been only to make much art more remote, obscure and unfathomable. In another essay, *The Author as Producer*, he stresses the need for socialist writers and artists to take full advantage of the potential of the new possibilities of reproduction, and to use them consciously to political effect. There is no guarantee of changing people's thought merely through the ready availability of works of art.

Lucien Goldmann (1913–1970)

Lucien Goldmann was a Romanian by birth but lived in France. He rejected the notion of individual genius in the arts. He believed that works of art and literature reflected the 'mental structures' of the class which engendered them. Great writers possessed the ability to formulate and express these structures and enable people to perceive them through the works. He developed a distinctive form of Marxist literary theory he called 'genetic structuralism' which, as the name suggests, also owes much to structuralist thought. He was interested in tracing the relationships between a work of literature, predominant modes of philosophical thought and ideology and specific social classes. There may be no obvious surface parallels but they share structural similarities on a deeper level. For this process of comparing parallel deep structures he used the term 'homology'. His most famous working out of the procedure was in his study of the French dramatist Racine (*Le Dieu Caché*). In *Pour une Sociologie du Roman* (1964), he provided a 'homological' study of the modern novel compared with the structure of market economy.

Louis Althusser (1918–1990)

Louis Althusser's ideas are also clearly indebted to structuralism. He abhorred the notion of order and systems with central controlling principles. Social structures consist of various levels in complex interaction with each other and often in mutual conflict. One level may dominate the rest at any time but this is itself determined by economic factors. In *A Letter on Art*, Althusser considers art to be located somewhere between ideology and scientific knowledge. A work of literature he sees in a somewhat negative light: it neither provides a full understanding of the real world, nor does it simply lend expression to the ideology of a specific class. But it does make us aware of the ideology which governs both its and our own existence in society.

In fact, Althusser presents in his writing two theses concerning ideology. The first is that, 'Ideology represents the imaginary relationship of individuals to their real conditions of existence'. The second thesis relates ideology to its social origins. For Althusser ideology works through the so-called 'ideological state apparatuses'. These include the political system, the law, education, organised religion etc. Ideology has a material existence in the sense that it is embodied in material systems. Thus, everything we do and everything we involve ourselves in is, in some way, ideological. When we believe that we are acting according to free will it is really in accordance with the dominant ideology. In accordance with his belief that social structures are not systems with central controlling principles, he also asserted that ideology in capitalist societies was not dominated by the self-interest of a small group who use it to exploit others. Those who profit from the system are as blind to its effects as others. One of the causes of this blindness is the very force of ideology itself. It convinces us that we are real 'concrete subjects'. We see as natural whatever ideology wants us to see as part of the natural order of things.

Critics influenced by Althusser's ideas have attempted

to show how, in novels, readers are often invited to become part of a world which is depicted as essentially free, peopled by individuals who behave in autonomous ways. Such novels also give the reader the illusion that he or she is free when, in fact, they are also in the grip of an ideology. Many Marxist critics, however, have not been happy with the implied deterministic view of ideology set down by Althusser. He seems to allow no scope for non-ideological thought or action.

Antonio Gramsci (1891–1937)

The Italian Marxist Antonio Gramsci did not contribute specifically to literary theory but his ideas have influenced many Marxist literary critics, notably the British critic Raymond Williams. Gramsci's concept of ideology is less deterministic than that of Althusser and allows room for dissent. Writing in the 1930s in Fascist Italy, Gramsci was fully aware of the power of ideology and of 'the consent given by the great masses of the population to the general direction imposed on social life by the dominant fundamental group'. For Gramsci, it was possible for the individual to resist what he called the 'hegemony': the domination by a ruling ideology through 'consent' rather than 'coercive power'. Under 'hegemony' the citizens of a state have internalised what the rulers want them to believe so thoroughly that they genuinely believe that they are expressing their own opinions. But this hegemony does not, as Althusser believed, blind all members of the society to the truth of the situation. It is possible to become aware of the dominance of 'hegemony' and resist its effects, even if it is impossible to escape completely its influence. This is the loophole of which the artist can take advantage.

Pierre Macherey

Another important influence on British critics in the 1960s and 1970s was Pierre Macherey. In *A Theory of Literary Production* (1966), Macherey considered a text not as something 'created' but as 'produced'. Whatever authorial intentions might be and whatever aesthetic standards might prevail at a given time, the literary text is never completely 'aware of what it is doing'. He regarded literary texts as being pervaded by ideology and it was the job of the critic to look for the cracks and weaknesses in the surface of the work, caused by its own internal contradictions. The title of a later essay summarises this view as *The Text Says What It Does Not Say*. In order to reveal the ideology in a text the critic must focus on what the text represses rather than overtly expresses. The cracks are the gaps where the author failed to make a thought conscious. To some extent, this approach pre-figures that of poststructuralism but, whereas Macherey considered his approach to be scientific and leading to objectively true interpretations, poststructuralists believed that there was no such thing as objective truth.

Raymond Williams (1921–1988)

The British critic Raymond Williams took as his task a complete reassessment of the British tradition of cultural thought. In *Culture and Society 1780–1950* (1958), he defined culture as 'a whole way of life'. He was very much aware that in any given society there is more than one single culture, each with its own 'ideas of the nature of social relationship'. The coexistence of different cultures does not mean that there cannot also be a common culture: '...there is both a constant interaction between these ways of life and an area which can properly be described as common to or underlying both.' While granting the 'vital importance' of literature, he was instrumental in establishing a broader base for cultural studies: 'For experience that is formally recorded we go, not only to the rich source of literature, but also to history, building, painting, music, philosophy, theology and social theory, the physical theory, the physical and natural sciences, anthropology, and indeed the whole body of learning.' Williams' work is sometimes compared and contrasted with his contemporary Richard Hoggart, who also broadened the base of literary studies to include popular literature. Hoggart has a warm engaging style and a strong sympathy for working class culture, as evidenced in his study *The Uses of Literacy: Aspects of Working-Class Life with Special Reference to Publications and Entertainments* (1957). A major difference between Hoggart and Williams is that of the nature of their political commitment. Williams' approach was determinedly historical and materialist and in fact he eventually described it as 'cultural materialism'. It was only in *Marxism and Literature* (1977) that he finally identified himself as a Marxist.

Terry Eagleton (1943–)

In *Criticism and Ideology* (1976), the British critic Terry Eagleton revealed the influence of Pierre Macherey's concern to find the cracks and contradictions in a text. In this early work, Eagleton was interested not in what made a text coherent but what made it incoherent. The influence of Althusser is also evident. There may be apparent freedom in a text but it is not free in its reflection of the dominant ideology. In this work Eagleton analysed a number of canonical British novels, exploring the relationships between literary form and ideology.

In the late 1970s Eagleton was greatly influenced by poststructuralism. He came to believe that deconstructive theories could be used to undermine all absolute forms of knowledge, although he also rejected the deconstructive denial of the possibility of objectivity. He now believed that it should be the role of the critic to analyse critically accepted notions of what constituted literature and reveal the ideologies behind them. He thought that the critic should interpret non–socialist works 'against the grain' to reveal a socialist perspective.

Eagleton shares with Walter Benjamin an admiration for Brecht. Benjamin admired Brecht's own re-reading of history 'against the grain', and this inspired Eagleton to devote a whole book to Benjamin: *Walter Benjamin or Towards a Revolutionary Criticism* (1981). Benjamin viewed history as always obscuring the significance of events by selective reactionary memory, and Brecht made audiences see history from the perspective of the downtrodden.

Eagleton's ideas undergo constant change. He has

utilised the psychoanalytic theories of Jacques Lacan and the ideas of Jacques Derrida. His own *Literary Theory, An Introduction* (1983, second edition 1996) provides a witty and perceptive analysis of major literary schools, concluding with doubts about the very viability of literary theory as an independent discipline. A recent book by Eagleton, *After Theory* (2003), takes a whole new perspective on the future of cultural theory. I shall take up some of these issues in my own final chapter.

Fredric Jameson

The American theorist Fredric Jameson has been greatly influenced by the Frankfurt School. He explored Marxist theories of literature, especially with reference to their dialectical aspects, in his *Marxism and Form* (1971). He returns, in fact, to a reconsideration of Hegel's philosophy, in its investigation of the part to the whole. Any object is bound up in a larger whole, is part, for example, of a specific historical situation. The aspects of literature that a critic analyses must also always be seen in relation to the critic's own historical situation.

In *The Political Unconscious* (1981), Jameson retains his earlier dialectic approach but also incorporates various other, often conflicting modes of thought, such as structuralism and poststructuralism. The influence of Althusser is also evident. Jameson sees ideologies as 'strategies of containment', providing acceptable explanations but suppressing contradictions. The solutions provided by works of literature also suppress historical truths. He also believes that the 'story' is an essential 'epistemological category' of the human mind. We can only understand the world in terms of stories. Scientific, cultural and historical accounts are all created narratives. Jameson took his title from Freud's concept of repression which he extends from the individual to the collective level: ideology represses revolutionary ideas. He provides a complex rethinking of Marxist thought about social structure and follows the view of Althusser that society is a 'decentred structure' in which various levels retain some degree of autonomy. The heterogeneity of society is reflected in the heterogeneity of texts: literature is essentially a mirror of the society in which it is produced. All kinds of interpretative methods can be applied to a text, and will reveal something actually present in the text but each method of interpretation applied will also reveal something about the ideologies governing both the author's and the critic's worlds. In *Postmodernism, or The Cultural Logic of Late Capitalism* (1991), Jameson maintains that postmodernism is not only a currently fashionable style but the 'cultural dominant', in Roman Jakobson's sense, of our times. It conditions the way we perceive and interpret our entire world.

Psychoanalysis

The Essence of Freudian Psychoanalysis

As with Marxism, it is impossible to do justice to the complexity of Freudian theory in the small scope of this book. Those aspects alone which are of direct relevance to literary theory will be summarised here. It must be said at the outset that much that passes for psychoanalysis of literature often uses the concepts, terminology and methodology very loosely. Be that as it may, a whole range of literary analysis and theory has now come to be termed psychoanalytic by virtue of its practitioners proclaiming it so. Certain concepts and views on mental processes must be held in common for the term psychoanalysis to be justified. Sigmund Freud himself was quite clear about what those essential concepts are. In a short article for inclusion in an encyclopaedia, he stated, under the heading *The Corner-Stones of Psychoanalytic Theory*: 'The assumption that there are unconscious mental processes, the recognition of the theory of resistance and repression, the appreciation of the importance of sexuality and of the Oedipus complex – these constitute the principal subject-matter of psychoanalysis and the foundations of its theory. No one who cannot accept them should count himself a psychoanalyst.'

Psychoanalysis was very much the product of one man's mind, although Freud gradually gathered many followers about him who shared his convictions and developed aspects of the theory further. He developed psychoanalysis in the first instance as a means of helping mentally disturbed patients. While studying under Charcot in Paris, he had become convinced of the existence of an extensive unconscious area of the mind which can, and does, wield strong influence over our conscious mind. Through close study of mentally disturbed patients and their symptoms he discovered that knowledge of the unconscious was accessible through analysis of dreams, symptomatic nervous behaviour and parapraxes (the famous Freudian slips). The conscious mind cannot cope with some of the unsavoury truths buried in the unconscious and, when they threaten to surface, represses them, attempting in practice to deny their reality. The tensions caused between the need of such truths to surface and the determination of the self to repress them can lead to serious mental disturbance, what Freud called neurosis, involving compulsive behaviour and obsessive modes of thinking. Cure was effected by helping the patient to understand what had brought about the behavioural disturbance and by tracing it to its roots in the unconscious. The most common, but not the only, needs repressed proved to be sexual in nature. Freud also developed a theory of the development of infantile sexuality and extended the areas of psychoanalytic interest to include broader cultural and social phenomena, including primitive beliefs, superstition, religion, the nature of civilisation etc.

He did not delineate a theory of art or aesthetics but

gave clear indications of how he saw art and literature fitting into a psychoanalytic scheme. Evidence for his views is spread throughout his writings and demonstrated in his frequent allusions to, and quotations from, works of literature. In his comments on E T A Hoffmann's story, *The Sandman*, in the essay *The Uncanny*, and in his comments on Shakespeare's *Richard III* and Ibsen's *Rosmersholm*, he hinted at lines of analysis rather than followed them through. His one extensive study of a work of literature was of the novella *Gradiva* by Wilhelm Jensen, which happens to lend itself very well to a Freudian analysis. Many theorists and critics assume too readily that Freud equated creative writing with dreaming and the outpourings of neurotics, largely because they rely too much on the opinions expressed in one essay: *Creative Writers and Daydreaming*. In fact, Freud clearly regarded the artist as a unique individual who avoids neurosis and sheer wishful thinking through the practice of his or her art. The artist or writer is involved in a process of sublimation (refining basic drives, such as those of sex and aggression, and converting them into creative and intellectual activity). Art is not an escape but a means of dealing with inner contradictions and re-establishing a productive relationship with the world. A good writer enables his/her readers to establish a similar relationship to their world, often in a new and critical light. Art is an illusion but its effects are real: 'Art is a conventionally accepted reality in which, thanks to artistic illusion, symbols and substitutes are able to provoke real emotions.' (*The Claims of Psychoanalysis to Scientific Interest*).

The best model for a psychoanalytic aesthetics in

Freud's own writings is his work *Wit and its Relation to the Unconscious* (1905). This study of wit (sometimes translated as 'Jokes') explores not only the psychological state of the person being witty but also explains how wit affects the audience and why consideration of the social context is important. In creating and enjoying wit, we share a critique of the social suppression of instincts. Wit, as an aesthetic phenomenon, is very far from being a form of consolation or reconciliation. It enlightens us and enables to share in protest against the self-denial we have accepted as the cost of a civilised existence.

Jacques Lacan (1901–1981)

Jacques Lacan has greatly influenced recent psychoanalytic theory in general as well as literary theory in particular. He broadened and redefined several basic psychoanalytic concepts in ways with which many orthodox Freudians disagree. According to Freud, in the earliest phase of childhood, the individual is dominated by the 'pleasure principle', seeking unreflecting gratification, with no definitely established identity and gender. Eventually, the child comes up against the restrictions of the father. (In pure Freudian terms this involves preventing the child from realising Oedipal desires for its mother by threatening it with castration. All this, of course, takes place on a subconscious level.) The father thus comes to represent the 'reality principle', forcing the child to heed the requirements of the real world for the first time. Identifying with the father now makes it possible for the child to take on a masculine role and

makes it aware for the first time of various forms of insti-
tutionalised law. The female child passes through slightly
different stages in the Freudian scheme of things, which
have been fundamentally criticised by many feminist
writers. The personality is then split between the
conscious self and repressed desire.

Lacan describes the earlier state of being, when the
child is unaware of any distinctions between subject and
object, as the 'imaginary'. Then comes the 'mirror phase',
when the child starts to become aware of itself as an individual (as though seeing an image of itself in a mirror) and
identifies this self. It produces something identifiable as an
ego. When it becomes aware of the father's restrictions, it
enters the 'symbolic' world and also becomes aware of
binary oppositions: male/female, present/absent etc.
Behind all this, the restricted desire persists.

Lacan then basically reinterprets Freud's theory of the
conscious and the unconscious in terms of Saussure's
theory of 'signifiers' and 'signifieds'. Entering the symbolic
order of consciousness, the child starts to link 'signifiers' and
'signifieds': developing language, in fact. The signifier 'I'
however is never fully comprehensible and, like other signifiers, never fully corresponds to 'signifieds'. To use Lacan's
metaphor, 'signifieds' slide under 'floating signifiers'.

The whole of Freud's dream theory is also reinterpreted
by Lacan as a textual theory, using Jakobson's concepts of
'metaphor' and 'metonymy' to explain the various struc-
turing principles defined by Freud, such as 'displacement'
(transferring emphasis from one element in a dream to
another), 'condensation' (combining several ideas and
images) and so on. The general effect of Lacan's theories

has been to sow seeds of doubt in the minds of many thinkers and writers about the ability of language to express anything with certainty. Meaning, especially in many modernist literary works, has become elusive and difficult, if not impossible, to pin down.

For Lacan, the whole of human life is like a narrative in which significance constantly eludes us. Consciousness starts out with a sense of loss (of the mother's body), and we are constantly driven by a desire to find substitutes for this lost paradise. All narrative can, in fact, be understood in terms of a search for a lost completion.

Another important concept in Lacanian thought is that of 'The Other'. This refers to the developing individual's awareness of other beings, who are also necessary in defining the individual's identity. 'The Other' is clearly a general concept for the entire social order. As the social context of every individual's life is constantly changing, however, so is the individual's sense of identity. It is always a process, never a state. Ideology is also part of 'The Other' and provides a 'misrecognition' of the self, a false interpretation which nevertheless becomes part of the self. But ideology gives us the illusion of filling the lack that desire is eternally seeking to fill, which is why it always has such a firm hold over us. When we read a literary text too, we allow it to dominate us in a similar way and to fill the lack in our being.

To read a text by Lacan is itself to be in constant pursuit of the obscure object of desire. Lacan's writing is at the other end of the spectrum from Freud's, whose clarity and clear argument won him the Goethe prize for good style in scientific writing.

The Psychoanalysis of Reader Response

Some critics have applied a psychoanalytic approach to the kind of satisfaction a reader feels when reading a work of literature. This may be interesting but it is rather limited in the insights it yields. The American Norman N Holland, in *The Dynamics of Literary Response* (1968), argues that we enjoy a work of literature because it enables us to work through deep anxieties and desires in ways which remain socially acceptable. Literature allows a compromise, which placates moral and aesthetic norms, while allowing realisation of what would normally remain repressed. This is little more than a restatement of Freud's own views in *The Creative Writer and Daydreaming*. Simon Lesser, in *Fiction and the Unconscious* (1957), had already pursued a similar line, presenting literature as a form of therapy. In Holland's book *Five Readers Reading* (1975), he explores how readers adapt their identities in the course of interpreting a text and discover a new unity within themselves.

Harold Bloom (1930–)

Harold Bloom applied psychoanalysis to the actual history of literature, interpreting developments and changes in styles and norms, in poetry in particular, as the result of a conflict between generations, akin to that envisioned in the Freudian Oedipus complex. As sons feel oppressed by their fathers, so do poets feel themselves to be in the shadow of influential poets who came before them. Any poem can be read as an attempt to shake off the 'anxiety of influence' of earlier poems. Poets reconstruct and reform earlier poems. Therefore, all poems can be considered to be rewritings of older poems, as deliberate 'misreadings' (or what Bloom calls 'misprisions') of them, to assert the younger poet's own individuality in face of them. These ideas found expression in Bloom's *A Map of Misreading* (1975), in which he was very much going beyond the implications of psychoanalysis. The work is already very much poststructuralist in its concerns. In it a poem is seen as containing a series of undermining devices. He also explicitly attacks deconstructive criticism, which he regards as 'serene linguistic nihilism', and endeavours to reaffirm the notion of author's intention. For Bloom, criticism is itself a form of poetry and poems incorporate literary criticism of other poems. It is one poetic and critical continuum.

Julia Kristeva (1941–)

Julia Kristeva combines Lacanian psychoanalysis with politics and feminism. In her book *La Révolution du langage poétique* (1974), Kristeva redefines and renames Lacan's concept of the 'imaginary' from a feminist perspective. In the Lacanian scheme, when the child enters the 'symbolic' phase and starts naming things and heeding principles of order and law, its whole existence takes as its centre the 'transcendental signifier', the phallus, the father as embodiment of law. Kristeva wishes to destroy the omnipotence of this male order. She posits a form of language as existing already in Lacan's 'imaginary' pre-Oedipal stage, which she calls instead the 'semiotic' stage. The 'semiotic' is a vague almost mystical concept. The underlying 'semiotic' flow is artificially broken up into units when the 'symbolic' order is imposed on it, but it persists as a kind of force within language. It is clearly associated with an essential femininity but it also occurs in a period of development when no distinctions of gender have yet taken place.

Kristeva finds confirmation of her theories not only in the ill-formed language of children and the language used by the mentally ill but also in certain kinds of poetry, such as that of the French Symbolists, in whose language, she argues, ordinary language is stretched to the limits of its conventionally accepted meanings. Such works, and such criticism, are essentially anarchic, a reaction against fixed signifiers of power, order and control, everything that is in any way associated with masculine dominance. All clear distinctions are broken down, as are all binary oppositions. There seems to be in her writing an assumption that the anarchy created by her mode of reading texts also implies a political anarchy, and thereby a political critique. Terry Eagleton has revealed this to be a rather naïve and simplistic notion of the political: '…she pays too little attention to the political *content* of a text, the historical conditions in which its overturning of the signified is carried out…'

Carl Gustav Jung (1875–1961)

Strictly speaking C G Jung is not a psychoanalyst but what he himself preferred to call an analytical psychologist. He is included here, however, for three important reasons: his theories have been very influential in the interpretation of literature; they have a lot more in common with Freud's theories than either of them would have been willing to admit; and they do not really fit into any other broad category utilised in this book.

It has become commonplace to stress the differences between Freud's and Jung's theories but it must also be remembered that, when compared to other kinds of psychological theory, they can be shown to share many common fields of interest: the study of schizophrenia, neuroses and psychoses, the nature of psychological complexes, the interpretation of dreams, and unconscious mental processes in general, to name only the most important fields.

Freud and Jung differed especially over the so-called libido theory. Jung thought that Freud related libido (the Latin for 'desire' or 'lust') too closely to sexual drives. He preferred the notion of 'psychic energy'. He developed a general theory of character types, broadly defined, in two terms which have entered common parlance, as extroverted and introverted personality types. Jung also believed in the existence of a collective unconscious, which is common to the whole human race and contains universal archetypes. These are primordial and universal images, revealed in dreams, artistic and literary productions, primitive religions and mythologies. One of the most important archetypes is that of the animus/anima. The animus is a woman's archetypal image of man and the anima is the man's archetypal image of woman. The animus often appears as a wise old man, and the anima as a virginal girl or a mother goddess. The general aim of

Jungian psychology is what he called 'individuation', a process by which the individual is helped to harmonise his/her 'persona' (the self as presented to the world) and 'the shadow' (the darker potentially dangerous side of the personality that exists in the personal unconscious). It could be said that the failure of individuation is represented symbolically in Robert Louis Stevenson's famous story *Dr. Jekyll and Mr. Hyde*, in which Dr Jekyll is the 'persona' and Hyde is 'the shadow'.

Jungian psychology has contributed little to the study of literature as text, but much to the interpretation of symbols and images in texts. The Jungian theory of archetypes has been influential on the French philosopher of science and literary theory Gaston Bachelard. He combined Freud's views on daydreaming with Jung's conception of archetypes in *The Poetics of Reverie* (1960). The theory of archetypes was also taken up by the Canadian literary theorist Herman Northrop Frye in his book, *Anatomy of Criticism* (1957).

Hermeneutics and Reception Theory

There is a continuum of a mode of theory from Hermeneutics to Reception Theory and both are based in a particular kind of philosophy which flourished in the early twentieth century, in Germany especially, known as phenomenology.

Phenomenology

This mode of philosophising has its roots in the dominant debates about the nature of knowledge stemming from the works of Immanuel Kant (1724–1804), and especially from Kant's distinction between phenomenon (the world as we perceive it) and noumenon (the world as it really is). Between the two World Wars, the German philosopher Edmund Husserl developed a philosophy in which he rejected common sense notions that objects exist 'objectively' outside our perception of them. We cannot claim this with any degree of certainty. Whether they are illusions or not, we can only be certain of how they appear to us. They are not 'things in themselves' (to use Kant's term), but are things posited by us. Consciousness is not just passive but actually conditions the world. The external world is, in a sense, reduced to the contents of our own

consciousness. Not surprisingly, because of its concentra-
tion on our experience of phenomena, this mode of
philosophy is known as phenomenology.

However, what we are aware of in our minds could be
described as a stream of consciousness, which is chaotic.
Obviously, certainty cannot be founded on this.
Phenomenology, therefore, endeavours to discover a
system of universal essences behind the apparently
random and individual phenomena. This is clearly
indebted to Plato's concept of 'ideas' (or types, 'eidos'), and
Husserl calls the process 'eidectic abstraction'. Any mode
of thought (including literary theory), which claims to be
phenomenological, thus stresses what we can, in our experience of the world (or text), be sure of perceiving.

The immediate influence of this mode of thinking on
literary theory was on the so-called Geneva School of
Criticism, which flourished in the 1940s and 1950s. It led
to a mode of criticism akin to New Criticism. Especially
associated with the school were the Belgian Georges
Poulet, the Swiss Jean Starobinski and Jean Rousset, the
French critic Jean-Pierre Richard, and the professor of
German at the University of Zürich, Emil Staiger, a
leading light in the study of German language and culture
known as *Germanistik*. Phenomenological criticism aimed
to provide what Germans call a *textimmanent* analysis,
which considers only that for which there is indisputable
evidence in the text. The text is considered to be the
embodiment of the author's mind, which is the unifying
presence behind it. This does not imply consideration of
the author's biography, except in so far as aspects of it are
manifest in the work. Evidence of deep structures in the

author's mind are sought in the text and seen as reflecting how he experienced his world. The world experienced in a literary work does not correspond to the real world exactly, but is 'the world as lived' (the *Lebenswelt*) of the author. This also conforms to Husserl's use of language. Language reveals clearly and distinctly how we perceive the world. It conforms 'in a pure measure to what is seen in its full clarity'. This means that language reflects our perceptions of the world and not the world itself.

The philosopher Martin Heidegger, while being greatly influenced by his predecessor, breaks with this idealist phenomenological approach and situates human beings fully in a given historical existence (*Dasein*). For Heidegger, unlike Husserl, the world is not something we can analyse rationally, from the point of view of a disinterested, contemplative subject. We are bound up in the world and cannot get outside it. We can never fully objectify the reality of our own world.

Because we are bound up in the world from birth, we already share many assumptions with each other about the world. These assumptions Heidegger calls 'pre-understanding'. But a human being can never fully grasp his or her existence, because there is also always development and change in a forward direction. Soon the presently perceived relationship between the self and the world will be no more. We are constantly projecting ourselves forward and knowing the world in new ways.

For Heidegger, language is not just something we use to express ourselves. It has an existence separate from us. It too 'pre-exists' us. Humans participate in language and thereby become human. We know the world through language in the way in which we know how to use a 'tool': we know the functions and uses of things. Thus we often do not realise the significance of something until it no longer works for us, until it 'breaks'. We only become fully aware of what a telephone means to us when we are cut off, and we only become fully aware of the importance of language when it no longer works for us, for example, when we have had a stroke. This is clearly a similar notion to that of the formalist term 'defamiliarisation', and, for Heidegger, art provides such a 'defamiliarisation' of objects. Heidegger describes his philosophy as a 'hermeneutic of Being', and this use of the term 'hermeneutics' needs further clarification.

Hermeneutics

Hermeneutics means the science or art of interpretation. In this sense Freudian psychoanalysis can be called hermeneutics. In fact Freud called it a *Deutungskunst* (art of interpretation). Heidegger called his philosophy 'hermeneutical phenomenology', because it was concerned with interpreting experience in a historical context rather than with the nature of the perception of phenomena as such, in Husserl's sense. The term 'hermeneutic' was originally applied to the interpretation of religious texts but, in the course of the nineteenth century, it came to refer to the understanding of texts in general. Another German philosopher was to apply Heidegger's hermeneutic approach to the understanding of literary texts: Hans-Georg Gadamer.

I. Hans-Georg Gadamer (1900–)

In *Truth and Method* (1975), Gadamer argues that, whatever the intentions of its author, the meaning of a work of literature is never exhausted by consideration of them. A work is not static but passes through various cultural and historical contexts. This fact enables new and different meanings to be perceived in it, which could not have been perceived by its author, nor by its contemporary audience. There is no possibility of knowing a literary text in any pure context, 'as it is'. What a work communicates to us depends on what questions we put to it. It also depends on our ability to understand the historical context in which it was conceived and written. We can enter into the alien world of a past work of literature but we always assimilate it into our own world.

Gadamer also assumes the existence of a tradition, a mainstream, in which all good works of literature participate. In this sense parallels can be drawn with Leavisite views in Britain. He argues that there is an unbroken line of continuity with works of the past, established through custom and tradition, and even through prejudice. He thus allows an intuitive dimension to interpretation which is 'outside the arguments of reason'.

Hermenutic methodology has been mainly applied to what are historically recognised classics of literature. The work, the author, the historical context and interpretation, all form a circular argument of mutual confirmation: the 'hermeneutic circle'. There is also an assumption that the work of literature is an 'organic whole', in harmony with tradition and its own historical context.

II. E D Hirsch Jr

The American critic, E D Hirsch Jr, is a hermeneuticist in the tradition of Husserl's philosophy. He attacks radically the hermeneutics of Heidegger and Gadamer. However, he also shares some perspectives with Gadamer. In *Validity in Interpretation* (1967), Hirsch argues that there can be a number of different valid interpretations of a text but that all of them must be compatible with the author's intended meaning. He agrees with Gadamer that a work can mean different things to different people at different times, but he distinguishes between 'meaning' and 'significance'. Meanings remain unchanged but a work's significance can change as the historical context changes.

Hirsch does not make the assumption, however, that we can always know what the author's intentions were. They may now be undiscoverable but this does not alter his basic philosophical stance: that literary meaning is in some way absolute and resists change. The job of the critic is to reconstruct the 'intrinsic genre' of the text. By this he means the general aesthetic conventions and 'world view', which would have conditioned the author's intended meanings.

The problem with Hirsch's approach is that he assumes that meaning can exist apart from the language in which it is expressed. A further problem is that it is, in most cases, virtually impossible to make very clear distinctions between what a text meant for its author at the time of its inception and what it means to a modern critic. The line simply cannot be drawn.

Reception Theory

As its name implies, reception theory focuses on the way a work of literature is received by its readers. It examines the ways in which the reader involves him/herself in literature.

Readers may be unaware of the fact but in the process of reading they are constantly making hypotheses about the meaning of what they are reading. They make inferences, draw connections, fill in gaps etc. The text itself supplies a series of 'clues' or 'cues', which the reader uses to lend some coherence to the act of reading. As reading proceeds, our expectations and projections are modified by further discoveries in the text. Reading is not a linear process. We create a frame of reference, in which we attempt to work out our interpretation, but what comes later in the text may cause us to alter the original frame.

I. Wolfgang Iser (1926–)

In *The Act of Reading* (1978), Wolfgang Iser examined the 'strategies' used in building up a text and the 'repertoire' of themes and allusions utilised. To read and understand a work we must already be familiar with the codes it employs but with good, stimulating literature it is not just a question of re-interpreting familiar codes. An effective work of literature forces the reader to become critically aware of familiar codes, makes us question their validity. It is therefore yet another example of what the formalists called 'defamiliarisation'. For Iser, reading critically and perceptively makes us more critically aware of our self-

...ness. He grants the possibilities of different readers interpreting a work in different ways. For him, there is no one correct interpretation, but a valid interpretation must be internally consistent. The best interpretation is that which can account for the greatest number of compatible interpretations. And a valid interpretation must also be limited, defined by the text itself. It must be clearly an interpretation of this particular text and no others.

II. Hans-Robert Jauss

Hans-Robert Jauss is more concerned than Iser to situate the interpretation of a literary text in its historical context and, in this sense, has much in common with Gadamer. He has attempted to produce a new kind of literary history, focusing not on authors and literary movements, but on how literature was 'received' in various historical periods. The texts themselves are actually altered by the ways in which they are received in each period. Jauss uses the term 'horizon of expectations' to refer to the criteria which readers use in any given period when approaching a work of literature. It may be possible to establish a 'horizon of expectations' to evaluate how a work was interpreted when it first appeared but this does not establish a permanent or final meaning. It must also be remembered that a writer may write in accordance with expectations of his or her day but may also challenge them. This often happens with writers not greatly regarded in their day but very much admired in later ages. The aim of establishing the 'horizon of expectations' for a work is ultimately to allow a 'fusion of horizons', bringing together in a coherent whole all valid perceptions of it.

III. Stanley Fish (1938–)

The American critic Stanley Fish developed a form of reception theory, which he called 'affective stylistics'. He examined reader expectations on the level of the sentence, and argued that we use the same reading strategies in understanding both literary and non-literary texts. It is possible to analyse the way in which a reader proceeds, word for word, through a text. Of course, this overlooks the fact that readers often jump forward in their expectations, envisaging a particular form of sentence. Much is guessed or anticipated in advance. The actual experience of reading is not the same as the word for word analysis of an artificially imposed procedure. These views are very much characteristic of Fish's early ideas but, in a later work, *Is There a Text in This Class?* (1980), he tries to overcome the limitations of his earlier theory by arguing for a community of readers, sharing the same assumptions in the process of reading. This also makes it much easier, of course, to assert that the writer him/herself is part of such a community and can therefore be readily comprehended by it.

IV. Michael Riffaterre

In a well-known essay, Michael Riffaterre attacks Jakobson's and Lévi-Strauss' interpretation of Baudelaire's *Les Chats*. He shows that the linguistic features they claim to have discovered in the poem could not be perceived by a reader, however well-informed. Many features they focus on are not part of the poetic structure as experienced by the reader. The reading by Jakobson and Lévi-Strauss depends on knowledge of their technical terminology. In his *Semiotics of Poetry* (1978), Riffaterre argues that elements in a poem often depart from normal grammar. A reader must know how to deal with such ungrammatical factors and this means developing a special competence. He assumes the existence of a structural 'matrix', often a single sentence or phrase, which may not actually occur in the poem. It is rather like an ideal sentence and, as such, resembles the basic sentences assumed in Noam Chomsky's transformational grammar. This ideal sentence or phrase is modified in actual utterances or usage (what Riffaterre calls 'hypograms'). This mode of reading a poem is especially useful in interpreting poems which go against the rules of normal grammar (such as many of those by Emily Dickinson) but it is limited in its application and often leads to generalities which do not explain why any given poem is especially effective.

Feminist Theory

What unites the various kinds of feminist literary theory is not so much a specific technique of criticism but a common goal: to raise awareness of women's roles in all aspects of literary production (as writers, as characters in literature, as readers etc.) and to reveal the extent of male dominance in all of these aspects. Women's attempts to resist the dominance of a patriarchal society have a long history but the actual term 'feminism' seems not to have come into English usage until the 1890s. In general, feminist criticism has also attempted to show that literary criticism and theory themselves have been dominated by male concerns. In fact, some feminists have reacted against all theory as an essentially male-dominated sphere. Theory, for them, is associated with the traditional male/female binary opposition: theory being essentially in the male domain and embracing all that is impersonal and would-be objective. Against this, they have placed the female world of subjectivity and primal experience. There is general agreement among most authors that, apart from recent developments, feminist theory can be divided into two major stages: The First Wave and The Second Wave.

The First Wave

The earlier phase of modern feminist theory was very much influenced by the social and economic reforms brought about by the Women's Rights and Suffrage movements. Two writers in particular stand out in this period for first raising many of the issues which would continue to preoccupy later feminists: Virginia Woolf and Simone de Beauvoir.

I. Virginia Woolf (1882–1941)

Apart from her novels, Virginia Woolf also wrote two works which contributed to feminist theory: *A Room with a View* (1927), and *Three Guineas* (1938). In the former, Woolf considered especially the social situation of women as writers and, in the latter, she explored the dominance of the major professions by men. In the first work she argued that women's writing should explore female experience and not just draw comparisons with the situation in society of men. Woolf was also one of the earliest writers to stress that gender is not predetermined but is a social construct and, as such, can be changed. However, she did not want to encourage a direct confrontation between female and male concerns and preferred to try to find some kind of balance of power between the two. If women were to develop their artistic abilities to the full, she felt it was necessary to establish social and economic equality with men.

II. Simone de Beauvoir (1908–1986)

Simone de Beauvoir is famous not only as a feminist but as the life-long partner of the French philosopher Jean-Paul Sartre. She was a very active fighter for women's rights and a supporter of abortion. Her most influential book is, without doubt, *The Second Sex* (1949). In this work, she outlined the differences between the interests of men and women and attacked various forms of male dominance over women. Already in the Bible and throughout history Woman was always regarded as the 'Other'. Man dominated in all influential cultural fields, including law, religion, philosophy, science, literature and the other arts. She also clearly distinguished between 'sex' and 'gender', and wrote (famously) 'One is not born, but rather becomes, a woman.' She demanded freedom for women from being distinguished on the basis of biology and rejected the whole notion of femininity, which she regarded as a male projection.

The Second Wave

The second wave of feminist theory was very much influenced by the various liberationist movements, especially in America, in the 1960s. Its central concern was sexual difference. The theorists of this second wave criticised especially the argument that women were made 'inferior' by virtues of their biological difference to men. Some feminist critics, on the other hand, celebrated the biological difference and considered it a source of positive values which women could nurture, both in their everyday lives and in works of art and literature. Another area of debate has been the question of whether white women and men perceive the world in the same ways, and differently to black women. Another much disputed question has been whether there exists a specifically female language. This has arisen from the sense that one reason for the oppression of women has been the male dominance of language itself. Some feminists have decided not to challenge dominance directly but rather to celebrate all that has been traditionally identified as the polar opposite of maleness. All that is disruptive, chaotic and subversive is seen as female, in a positive, creative sense, in contrast to the restrictive, ordering and defining obsessions of maleness.

I. Kate Millett (1934–)

Kate Millett's book *Sexual Politics* (1969) was probably the most influential feminist work of its period. Her central argument is that the main cause of the oppression of women is ideology. Patriarchy is all-pervasive and treats females universally as inferior. In both public and private life the female is subordinate. Millett also distinguishes very clearly between 'sex' (biological characteristics) and 'gender' (culturally acquired identity). The interaction of domination and subordination in all relations between men and women is what she calls 'sexual politics'. Millett also reveals a special interest in literature, arguing that the very structure of narrative has been shaped by male ideology. Male purposiveness and goal-seeking dominate the structure of most literature. To show up the extent to which the perspectives in most works are those of the men, she deliberately provides readings of famous works of literature from a woman's perspective. However, she reveals a misconceived view of homosexuality in literature (especially in the works of Jean Genet), which she could only comprehend as a kind of metaphor for subjection of the female.

II. Sandra Gilbert (1936–) and Susan Guber (1944–)

Gilbert and Guber's *The Madwoman in the Attic* (1979) is famous for its exploration of certain female stereotypes in literature, especially those of the 'angel' and the 'monster'. The title refers to the mad wife whom Rochester has locked in the attic in Charlotte Brontë's *Jane Eyre*. They have been criticised for identifying many examples of patriarchal dominance without providing a thorough criticism of it.

III. Elaine Showalter (1941–)

One of the most influential books of The Second Wave is Elaine Showalter's *A Literature of their Own* (1977), which provides a literary history of women writers. It outlines a feminist critique of literature for women readers as well as identifying crucial women writers. She coined the term 'gynocriticism' for her mode of analysing the works of women writers. She also argues for a profound difference between the writing of women and that of men and delineates a whole tradition of women's writing neglected by male critics. She divides this tradition into three phases.

The first phase was from about 1840 to 1880, and she refers to it as the 'feminine' phase. It includes writers such as George Eliot and Elizabeth Gaskell. Female writers in this phase internalised and respected the dominant male perspective, which required that women authors remained strictly in their socially acceptable place. From this perspective, it is significant that Mary Anne Evans found it necessary to adopt the male pen name of 'George Eliot'. The Second Phase, the 'feminist' phase, from 1880 to 1920 included radical feminist writers who protested against male values, such as Olive Schreiner and Elizabeth Robins. The Third Phase, which she describes as the 'female' phase, developed the notion of specifically female writing. Rebecca West and Katherine Mansfield exemplify this phase.

IV. Julia Kristeva (1941–)

The central ideas of Julia Kristeva have already been outlined in relation to the influence of Lacanian psychoanalysis on her work. She considered Lacan's 'symbolic' stage in a child's development to be the main root of male dominance. When a child learns language, it also recognises principles of order, law and rationality associated with a patriarchal society. Lacan's pre-Oedipal 'imaginary' stage is referred to by Kristeva as 'semiotic', and literature, especially poetry, can tap the rhythms and drives of this stage. The pre-Oedipal stage is also associated very closely with the body of the mother. When the male child enters the 'symbolic' order, however, the child identifies with the father. The female child is identified with pre-Oedipal, pre-discursive incoherence, and is seen as a threat to the rational order. As has been already explained, Kristeva advocates a kind of anarchic liberation, in which 'poetic' and 'political' become interchangeable.

V. Helène Cixous (1937–)

Helène Cixous' essay, *The Laugh of the Medusa* (1976), argues for a positive representation of femininity in women's writing. Her mode of writing is often poetic rather than rational: 'Write yourself. Your body must be heard.' There is a paradox at the heart of Cixous' theory in that she rejects theory itself: '…this practice can never be theorized, enclosed, encoded – which doesn't mean that it doesn't exist.' Her notion of a specific *écriture féminine* is intended to subvert the symbolic rational 'masculine' language. Like Julia Kristeva, she also links *écriture féminine* to Lacan's pre-Oedipal 'imaginary' phase. She advocates also what she refers to as 'the other bisexuality', which actively encourages and relishes sexual differences. It must be said that her writing is full of contradictions: rejecting a biological account of the female but nevertheless celebrating the female body; including binary oppositions but denying their importance; encouraging a specifically female form of writing but celebrating pre-linguistic, non-verbal experience. It is a position which one is tempted to describe as full of much sound and fury but signifying, in both Saussurean and Shakespearean senses, nothing.

VI. Luce Irigaray (1932–)

Luce Irigaray is especially critical of Freud's view of women. In *Spéculum de l'autre femme* (1974) she argues that Freud's 'penis envy' envisages women as not really existing at all independently but only as negative mirror images of men. Male perception is clearly associated with sight (observation, analysis, aesthetics etc), but women gain pleasure from physical contact. The eroticism of women is fundamentally different to that of men. For Irigaray, all this implies that women should celebrate their completely different nature to men, their otherness. Only in this way can they overcome the traditional male-dominated perception of women.

VII. Ruth Robbins

The general concern of Marxist Feminism is to reveal the double oppression of women, both by the capitalist system and by sexuality within the home, and to explain the relationships between the two. The ideas of Ruth Robbins provide a good example of the combination of feminist concerns and Marxist principles. In *Literary Feminisms* (2000), she advocates a Marxist feminism which explains 'the material conditions of real people's lives, how conditions such as poverty and undereducation produce different signifying systems than works produced in conditions of privilege and educational plenty'.

Poststructuralism

The Essence of Poststructuralism

The name says everything and nothing. It comes after structuralism; it is a reaction against structuralism. But, in its critique of structuralism, it was not conducting a post-mortem. Structuralist influence continued to be very much alive and kicking. It was also a very complex phenomenon, which cannot be explained just by its relationship to structuralism. It must also be stressed that poststructuralism and deconstruction theory are parts of a continuum and that it is mainly for the sake of clarity that they have been allotted separate sections. Many of the theorists too are relevant, not only to poststructuralism and deconstruction theory, but also to psychoanalysis and feminism. Names such as Jacques Lacan, Paul de Man, Hélène Cixous, Julia Kristeva and others will recur. However, examining what poststructuralism found to be wrong with structuralism is as good a place to start as any. The great guru of the structuralists, Saussure, was about to be dethroned, because a signifier was no longer perceived as signifying anything any more. Or not quite as Saussure envisaged it, at least.

With every 'sign', Saussure had posited, 'signifier' and

'signified' were two sides of the same coin. Although they were in an arbitrary relationship, they stuck together through thick and thin. The word 'dog' and that furry creature there wagging its tail were permanently wed (at least, in the English language they were). Then poststructuralism came along and threw doubt on this whole cosy little arrangement. For them a 'sign' is a very temporary coming together of 'signifier' and 'signified': a one-night stand. The very dictionary itself, the fount of all certainty about language, proves the point. When you seek the meaning of a word in a dictionary you are indefinitely deferred. Look up that word 'dog' and you find 'a common four-legged animal, especially any of the many varieties kept by humans...' etc. Look up 'animal' and you find 'a living creature, not a plant.' Look up 'living creature'... and so on ad infinitum. For poststructuralists, signifiers form complex patterns of meaning with other signifiers and their meanings can never be pinned down. Many of these ideas are expounded in full by Jacques Derrida but, as he is closely associated with the concept of 'deconstruction', his ideas will be examined in that section.

Saussure's concepts of 'parole' (language as utterance) and 'langue' (language competence) were also under attack by the poststructuralists. Structuralists were interested primarily in 'langue', the deep structure which makes communication and meaning possible. But poststructuralists saw 'langue' as a kind of myth. Language does not have an impersonal structure underlying utterances. It is always and only an articulated system, which interacts with other systems of meaning and with human social existence. This concept of language poststructuralists prefer to call 'discourse'.

According to poststructuralists everything is discourse. Objective reporting of things and events in language is simply impossible. All language, meaning everything we can potentially say, pre-exists our utilisation of it. Subject and object cannot be sharply distinguished. This not only applies to our use of language but to all systems of knowledge, including science. New knowledge is attained when there is a jump from one accepted form of discourse to a completely new one, a paradigm-shift.

This blurring of the distinctions between subject and object also throws the whole notion of personal identity into doubt. When I use the pronoun 'I' or refer to myself as 'me', these are also signifiers which are unstable. It implies that 'I' can never be fully present to 'you', and consequently 'you' can never be fully present to 'me'. The notion of a stable, unified self is a fiction. Another interesting aspect of this is that, according to poststructuralists, when we speak we have a greater sense of being at one with the 'I' who speaks, than we do, when writing, with the 'I' who writes. Writing is second-hand, at one remove from consciousness. It is alienated from the self. This is why the identity of the 'I' in writing is always suspect. However, one should be cautious of granting this belief universal validity, as there are people who claim to be more at one with their self when writing than when speaking.

Roland Barthes (1915–1980)

A central tenet of Barthes' thought is that all forms of communication and representation are conventional. He despises the writer who deludes him/herself and his or her readers into thinking that language can be a transparent medium, through which it is possible to transmit clear unambiguous ideas or images of reality. A writer should be honest about the artificiality of what he or she is doing.

Something which characterises much poststructuralist thought is the occurrence of infinite regress or doubt. In *Elements of Semiology* (1967), Barthes expresses the belief that structuralism can be applied to all sign systems. However, he thinks that, by the same token, structuralism can also be subjected to a structural analysis, and indeed to other modes of analysis. Following upon this he cannot avoid the conclusion that metalanguages (processes of thought that reflect on other modes of thought or processes) can be subject themselves to analysis by other metalanguages ad infinitum. All forms of thought are by this token, therefore, fictions. No ultimate truth is ever discernible.

The most famous of Barthes' works is, undoubtedly, *The Death of the Author* (1968). In this essay, he rejects the view that an author is the originator of his text and the sole authority for its valid interpretation. A work in no way and on no level reflects an author's intentions concerning the work. The author is nothing more than the location where a verbal event takes place. The reader can therefore approach the text from any direction what-soever, and can interpret the text (the 'signifier') without respecting any intended meaning (the 'signified').

In *The Pleasure of the Text* (1975), Barthes pursues this self-indulgence on the part of the reader even further. For him, there are two kinds of pleasure to be gained in reading a text. The first is simple 'pleasure'. We feel this when we perceive something more than the simple and obvious meaning of what we read. We make an association, draw an inference, recall an image etc. This disrupts the linear flow of the text. Something, in a sense unjustified, is brought into association with the basic meanings of a text. We gain pleasure also from the rhythm of the narrative and from allowing our attention to wander. All this is acceptable and non-provocative in the context of normal cultural pursuits.

Barthes' second type of pleasure is what must appear to be an odd interpretation of the concept for most people. For many it is difficult to identify it as a kind of pleasure at all. The word he uses for it is *jouissance*, which means 'pleasure' in French, but which is usually translated as 'bliss', as he clearly envisages a stronger, virtually orgasmic form of pleasure. For Barthes, it is clearly something akin to the thrill of revolutionary feelings or actions. A text which provides a sense of 'bliss' 'unsettles the reader's historical, cultural, psychological assumptions'. It is the thrill of discovering the new, the dangerous, that which threatens chaos, anarchy. If the reader is not receptive to such an experience, he or she will feel only boredom but surrendering to it will bring the sense of 'bliss'. It seems a little like the effect which Franz Kafka required of a good book: that of an ice-axe breaking the frozen sea of the mind.

One of Barthes' most notorious books, which many consider to be his most impressive, is the oddly named *S/Z* (1970). In this work he starts with a thorough critique of structuralist attempts to trace common basic structures in all stories. He is more interested in what makes them different than what they have common. Every text refers back, in different ways, to all other texts that have ever been written. For Barthes, there are two types of text: that which allows the reader only to comprehend in a predetermined way and that which makes the reader into the producer of his or her own meaning. The first type of text he calls 'readerly' (*lisible*) and the other 'writerly' (*scriptible*). It is clear that Barthes prefers the second kind: 'this ideal text is a galaxy of signifiers, not a structure of signifieds.' It is possible for a reader to apply an infinite number of interpretations to such a text. None of them needs to be compatible nor part of an overall unity.

Barthes demonstrates his approach to actual texts by breaking down a novella by Honoré de Balzac (*Sarrasine*) according to specific codes. He first divides the story into a random number of reading units (581 'lexias'). Each of them is then subjected to analysis according to five codes:

1. Hermeneutic (relating to the enigma or mystery in the story).
2. Semic (relating to associations evoked).
3. Symbolic (relating to polarities and antitheses in the story).
4. Proairetic (relating to basic action and behaviour).
5. Cultural (relating to commonly shared cultural knowledge between text and reader).

The Balzac story is commonly regarded as a realist work and Barthes, in Terry Eagleton's words, 'drastically rewrites and reorganizes it out of all conventional recognition'. *Sarrasine* thereby becomes what Barthes terms a 'limit text' for literary realism. His analysis reveals the limits of the realist mode of writing.

Michel Foucault (1926–1984)

The post that Michel Foucault held at the Collège de France, Paris, at the time of his death, aptly sums up his unique specialist field: 'Professor of the History of Systems of Thought'. He can justifiably be described as poststructuralist in one important sense. The structuralists used linguistics as their model of analysis but Foucault considered this inadequate and focused instead on the history of social and political systems and discourses. Because of this, he has been very influential in the field of literary history. His concept of 'discourse' needs some clarification.

Foucault's use of the term 'discourse' is closely related to his concept of power. The power of the human sciences (eg psychology, economics etc) derives from their claims to be knowledge. They expect respect for their claims and thereby exert power and influence. Practitioners in these fields set themselves up as experts and it is through their claimed expertise that power is exerted. For Foucault, a discourse is a loose structure of interconnected assumptions which makes knowledge possible. He expounded this idea most clearly in his work *The Archaeology of Knowledge* (1972), in which he asserted that discourse can be defined as a large group of statements belonging to a single system of formation, what he calls a 'discursive formation'. He cites the examples of 'clinical discourse, economic discourse, the discourse of natural history, psychiatric discourse'. One of the main reasons why knowledge can be a form of power is that it is a method of defining and categorising other people. It leads eventually to disciplining those who do not conform or, in the case of psychiatry, those who are defined as unsocial or criminal. It also leads to surveillance, what Foucault calls 'panopticism'. This is realised, for example, in the form of policing and the setting up guards in prisons to observe every move of the inmates. Of course, when considering the latter part of the twentieth century, one might want to add the advent of widespread CCTV surveillance.

Foucault was greatly influenced by the German philosopher Friedrich Nietzsche and his concept of power. Nietzsche argued that all forms of knowledge are expressions of the 'Will to Power'. On this assumption it is not possible to assume the existence of absolute truths or any kind of objective knowledge. An idea or theory is only 'true' if it accords with notions of truth held by the prevailing authorities of the day, whether intellectual or political. For Foucault, what it is possible for an author to say changes from one period to another. What is considered normal or rational in any given period is confirmed by rules, tacit or otherwise. Those who do not abide by the rules are excluded from the prevailing discourse, and are either suppressed or condemned as mad. The education system is also important in institutionalising these rules and inculcating them into the minds of new generations.

Foucault points out that different forms of knowledge have arisen in different historical periods and been replaced eventually by new systems of thought. For him, history is such a series of disconnected discursive practices. Specifically he was interested in the fields of psychiatry, medicine, sex and crime. It must be stressed that the rules governing such discourses are not consciously employed. We can understand the bodies of discourse of earlier eras only because we are governed by different discourses and are remote from that era. As we view past discourses through our own unconscious discourses, we can never possess an objective knowledge of history.

The work of Foucault which deals most explicitly with writing and authorship is the essay *What is an Author?* (1969). In this essay, he recognises the importance of Barthes' essay *The Death of the Author* but views the question of authorship as being more complex. However, the idea of an ideal society in which literature could circulate anonymously appeals to him greatly. It would seem that, for Foucault, the aim of writing is not to express the self or to fix a meaning but to create an individual object behind which the writer can efface him or herself: 'Writing unfolds like a game that invariably goes beyond its own rules and transgresses its limits. In writing, the point is not to manifest or exalt the act of writing, nor is it to pin a subject within language; it is rather a question of creating a space into which the writing subject constantly disappears.'

In one sense, Foucault does consider the author to be dead, but this death is one in which the author is complicit. The author of fiction especially attempts to deny his or her presence (it would seem that Foucault is thinking of realist fiction in particular): 'Using all the contrivances that he sets up between himself and what he writes, the writing subject cancels out the signs of his particular individuality. As a result, the mark of the writer is reduced to nothing more than the singularity of his absence; he must assume the role of the dead man in the game of writing.'

Deconstruction

Deconstruction is unthinkable without poststructuralism. Many of the writers associated with poststructuralism are considered to have practised deconstruction. The same presuppositions are shared by both approaches. The purpose of the present section is to outline the specific characteristics of a deconstructive approach to literary analysis. The notion of deconstruction is indissolubly linked to the name of Jacques Derrida.

Jacques Derrida (1930–2005)

Like him or loathe him, Jacques Derrida is a force with which to be reckoned. One cannot take lightly a man who called into question the basic metaphysical assumptions of all western philosophy since Plato. The first signs of the revolution came in a paper given at the Johns Hopkins University, America, in 1966: *Structure, Sign and Play in the Discourse of the Human Sciences*. To express what was revolutionary about it in a nutshell: he argued that even structuralism assumes a centre of meaning of some kind, as individuals assume the central 'I' in their own consciousness. This centre guarantees a sense of unity of being. But, for Derrida, recent developments in western thought have led inevitably to a decentring process. Traditionally there have always been 'centring' processes: being, self, essence, God etc. This human need Derrida called 'logocentrism' (in his work *Of Grammatology*, 1976). This derives from the New Testament use of the term 'logos' (the Greek for 'word') to express the Christian belief that the primary cause of all things was the spoken word of God: 'In the beginning was the Word.' In 'logocentrism', the spoken word is thus closer to thought than the written word. This Derrida refers to as 'phonocentrism', which always presupposes the presence of self. When we hear speech, we assume a speaking presence. A writing presence is not assumed in the same way when we read writing. In this way writing lends itself more readily to reinterpretation, because we can reread and analyse it more easily.

These views have been accepted and unquestioned hitherto in western thought, but what Derrida then proceeds to do is to upset the ranking order of speech and writing and 'deconstruct' this whole way of thinking: both speech and writing share 'writerly' features, and both are signifying processes which lack a real sense of presence (of the speaker or writer). He makes the remarkable assertion that all speech is always already written. Essentially, nothing new is ever possible. He also develops the notion of a 'violent hierarchy'. By creating a hierarchy of speech over writing we do violence to the truth: when we say that 'a' is prior to 'b', in fact 'b' is already implied in 'a'. Thus the word 'good' implies the word 'evil', 'law' implies 'lawlessness' etc. A deconstructive reading of a text identifies the existence of such hierarchies, reverses them and ultimately demonstrates that neither of the pair of opposites in each case is superior to the other: they are interdependent.

In Derrida's approach to literary analysis there is the assumption that all texts, whether literary or not, can be deconstructed. This involves, in effect, dismantling texts, or parts of them, to reveal inner inconsistencies: where a text might appear to imply one thing, it can, in fact, be shown to imply its opposite. Texts create only a semblance of stable meaning. Where a text may appear to offer the reader options (either/or), in fact, it offers no such choice (both/and), and remains ultimately uncommitted, leaving the reader with no sense of closure. The kinds of options which a text offers will often be in the form of apparent binary oppositions which the text seems to distinguish. These include distinctions such as self and non-self, conscious and unconscious, truth and falsity, reason and madness etc. Derrida's actual technique is to focus on points in a text where contradictions are evident (symptomatic points) and pursue the implications of these points, eventually undermining (deconstructing) the whole edifice.

It is not surprising that Derrida chose to apply his approach to a short story, Franz Kafka's *Before the Law*, which most critics have always agreed offers no closure (it did not need deconstruction to reveal this to us!). In the story a man arrives at a door that gives him access to the Law. He is not allowed to enter but is told by the doorman that he may perhaps enter later. He waits all his life and finally, just before he dies, he asks the doorman why he has been the only one to have sought admittance. The doorman tells him that that particular door was meant only for him and he shuts the door as the man dies. For Derrida the story contains an endless deferment of meaning ('différance'): 'Deferment till death, and for death, without end because ended, finite. As the door-keeper represents it, the discourse of the law does not say "no" but "not yet", indefinitely.' For Derrida, any given text involves such endless deferment of meaning, although it may not be so clearly evident as in the Kafka story.

As indicated already, Derrida made his first public declaration of his deconstructive credo at an American university, and it was American literary critics who first applied deconstruction more extensively to literary texts. Significant among them were Paul de Man and J Hillis Miller. Harold Bloom can also be described as decon-structive, but his ideas have implications also for psycho-analytic literary criticism and he has been discussed in that context. It should also be remembered that Barthes' analysis of the Balzac story in *S/Z* (see the section on poststructuralism) is essentially deconstructive in its reve-lation of contradictions in the text.

Paul de Man (1919–1983)

The American critic Paul de Man has applied decon-struction to Romantic poets and he argues, in fact, that the Romantics actually deconstructed their own writing by revealing that the desired presence (what is yearned for) in their poetry is always absent or deferred, always in the past or the future. Fulfilment is eternally deferred (as exemplified most vividly in Keats' *Ode To A Grecian Urn*:

'She cannot fade, though thou hast not thy bliss,/ For ever wilt thou love, and she be fair!'). De Man explained his methodology in two works in particular: *Blindness and Sight* (1971) and *Allegories of Reading* (1979). He also employs his own terminology which is different to that of Derrida. The first book proposes the notion that critics only achieve insight through a certain blindness to aspects of what they are doing. For example New Criticism based its approach on a concept of organic form, but in fact demonstrated how ambiguous meanings are. They created a 'hermeneutic circle' of interpretation which they mistook for unity within the work itself. In *Allegories of Reading* de Man analyses the use of figures of speech (tropes) by means of which writers say one thing but mean another (as in metaphor and metonymy). He argues that figures of speech destabilise the conventional logic of thought and he believes that language is basically figurative and cannot ultimately refer to or express non-linguistic realities. All language is therefore essentially rhetorical.

De Man is in danger of succumbing to the infinite regress of Barthes' metalinguistic account of a metalanguage. This is because, for him, critical writing itself is essentially comparable to a figure of speech: allegory. It is a sign sequence which is itself removed from another sign sequence (the text) and attempts to replace it in the reader's perception. Reading a text is therefore only a 'misreading'. But de Man believes that some 'misreadings' are correct and others incorrect. A correct misreading does not repress the unavoidable 'misreadings' of the text: it recognises them. For him in fact every literary text is self-deconstructing. It 'asserts and denies the authority of its own rhetorical mode'. This approach to criticism seems to set up as an ideal model a kind of infinite quibbling: a never-ending series of qualifications of meaning which results in a useless nihilism. Terry Eagleton has argued that this 'bottomless linguistic abyss' is brought about by suspending the reader between literal and figurative meanings of a text, in a way which makes commitment to one interpretation impossible. Literature for de Man is less deluded than other forms of writing, because it is essentially ironic, and being conscious of the fact constantly deconstructs itself.

J Hillis Miller

J Hillis Miller, also an American, was greatly influenced by phenomenological criticism (as in *Fiction and Repetition: Seven English Novels* 1982). He was also greatly indebted to Jakobson's theory of metaphor and metonymy, although, in effect, he deconstructs Jakobson's original opposition of metaphor (which is essentially poetic) and metonymy (which is essentially realistic). Miller argues that poetry is often read as though it were realistic and would-be realistic writing can be shown to be a fiction. But many have criticised Miller for his implication that language can never refer to the actual world.

Postcolonial Theory

For the purposes of the study of literature the most relevant concern of postcolonial thought has been the decentralisation of western culture and its values. Seen from the perspective of a postcolonial world, it has been the major works of thought of Western Europe and American Culture that have dominated philosophy and critical theory as well as works of literature throughout a large part of the world, especially those areas which were formerly under colonial rule. Derrida's concept of a 'white mythology', which has attempted to impose itself on the entire world, has lent support to the postcolonial attack on the dominance of western ideologies. The postmodern rejection of 'grand narratives', universalising western modes of thought, has also been very influential (see the section on postmodernism). The most important writers among postcolonial theorists are Edward Said, Homi Bhabha and G C Spivak.

Edward Said (1935–)

Said is concerned to relate poststructuralist theories of discourse, especially that of Foucault, to real political problems in the world. His most important work in this respect is *Orientalism* (1978). Said distinguishes between three usages of the term 'orientalism'. Firstly, it refers to the long period of cultural and political relations between Europe and Asia. Secondly, the term is used to refer to the academic study of oriental languages and culture which dates from the early nineteenth century. And thirdly, it is used to refer to the stereotypical views of the Orient developed by many generations of western writers and scholars, with their prejudiced views of orientals as inherently criminal and deceitful. He includes evidence, not only from literature, but also from such sources as colonial government documents, histories, studies of religion and language, travel books etc. The distinction between 'the Orient' and 'the Occident' exists, in Said's view, only in 'imaginative geography'. Said's analyses of various social discourses are therefore essentially deconstructive and 'against the grain'. His aim is to 'decentre' awareness of the 'Third World' and provide a critique which undermines the dominance of 'First World' discourses.

For Said, all the representations of the Orient by the West constituted a determined effort to dominate and subjugate it. Orientalism served the purposes of western hegemony (in Gramsci's sense): to legitimize western imperialism and convince the inhabitants of such regions that accepting western culture was a positive civilising process. In defining the East, orientalism also defined what the West conceived itself to be (in the way of binary oppositions). Stressing the sensuality, primitiveness and despotism of the East underlined the rational and democratic qualities of the West. In the light of Said's theories, literature written by native populations could now be seen in a new light. Did the writers comply with western hegemony or oppose it? In his essay, *The World, the Text and the Critics* (1983), Said criticised all modes of textual analysis which considered texts as being separate from the world in which they exist. The notion of it being possible for there to be infinite possible readings of a text could only be entertained by such severing of the text from the real world.

Homi Bhabha (1950–)

Homi Bhabha is essentially interested in exploring non-canonical texts which reflect the margins of society in a postcolonial world. He explores the subtle interrelations between cultures, the dominant and the subjugated. Of especial interest to him is the way in which subjugated races mimic their subjugators. These ideas are explored especially in the volume *The Location of Culture* (1994). There are examples of such 'mimics' in several well-known works of literature which trace the relations between the British and the Indians: in the works of Rudyard Kipling, such as *Kim*, and in E M Forster's *A Passage to India*. They exist in between cultures and, neither fully of the one nor of the other, are in fact hybrids.

Bhabha argues that the interaction between coloniser and colonised leads to the fusion of cultural norms, which confirms the colonial power but also, in its mimicry, threatens to destabilise it. This is possible because the identity of the coloniser is inherently unstable, existing in an isolated expatriate situation. The coloniser's identity exists by virtue of its difference. It materialises only when in direct contact with the colonised. Before that, its only reality is in the ideology of orientalism, as defined by Said.

G C Spivak (1942–)

Spivak has been described as the first truly feminist post-colonial theorist. She criticises western feminism especially for focusing on the world of white, middle-class heterosexual concerns. She is also interested in the role of social class and has focused on what in postcolonial studies has become known as the 'subaltern', originally a military term referring to those who are in a lower rank or position. Its usage in critical theory is derived from the writings of Gramsci. Spivak uses the term to refer to all the lower levels of colonial and postcolonial society: the unemployed, the homeless, subsistence farmers etc. Of course, she is especially interested in the fate of the 'female subaltern'. She is concerned that the 'female subaltern' is not misrepresented (in *Can the Subaltern Speak?* 1988). Spivak argues that, in the traditional Indian practice of burning widows on the funeral pyres of their husbands, neither the Indians nor the British colonisers allowed the women themselves to express their own views. She combines Marxism and a deconstructive approach in analysis of colonialist texts, showing how they create false oppositions between a united colonialist consciousness and a fictional primitive chaos. It is possible, she argues, through deconstruction of the text, to reveal the instability of these oppositions, the hollowness in fact of the colonial power structure.

Postmodernism

One of the most problematic aspects of postmodernism is the term 'postmodernism' itself. It is difficult to find agreement among critics on its range of meanings and implications. One can only familiarise oneself with the range and note the overlaps. Some critics understand postmodernism to be essentially a later development of modernist ideas, but others regard it as radically different. Some believe it possible to consider writers and artists in the pre-modern period as essentially postmodern, even though the concept was not yet conceived. This is akin to the argument which sees Freud's theories of the unconscious prefigured in German Romantic thought. The German philosopher Jürgen Habermas has argued that the 'project of modernity' is far from over and continues to pursue its goals (by this he means the Enlightenment values of reason and social justice). The term 'postmodernism' (and its cognates) is also often considered by many to refer, in general, to the role of the media in late twentieth century capitalist societies. Whatever usage one prefers, it is clear that 'postmodernist theory' implies certain critical stances: that the attempts to explain social and cultural developments by means of 'grand narratives' (all-embracing theories or accounts) are no longer feasible or acceptable, and that ideas can no longer be closely related to a historical reality. All is text, image, simulation. The world envisaged in the film *The Matrix*, one in which all human life is a simulation controlled by machines, is, for many of a postmodernist persuasion, not a science fiction nightmare but a metaphor for the present human condition.

These stances imply a fundamentally sceptical attitude to all human knowledge and have affected many academic disciplines and fields of human endeavour (from sociology to law and cultural studies, amongst others). For many postmodernism is dangerously nihilistic, undermining all sense of order and central control of experience. Neither the world nor the self have unity and coherence.

Postmodern writing, as postmodern thought, unsettles and destabilises all traditional notions about language and identity. Foreign students of English literature have been heard, frequently, to describe as 'postmodern' anything they cannot understand or express. Postmodern literary texts frequently reveal an absence of closure and analyses of them focus on that absence. Both texts and critiques are concerned with the uncertainty of identity and what is known as 'intertextuality': the reworking of earlier works or the interdependence of literary texts.

Postmodernism has attracted both strong positive and negative criticism. It can be seen as a positive, liberating force, destabilising preconceived notions of language and its relation to the world and undermining all metalanguages about history and society. But it is also seen as undermining its own presuppositions and warding off all coherent interpretation. For many it is apolitical and ironically non-committal.

A genre popular with postmodernist writers is that of parody, which enables the simultaneous recognition and breaking down of traditional literary modes. Postmodern writers break down boundaries between different discourses, between fiction and non-fiction, history and autobiography (a prime example of this is the writings of W G Sebald). Two thinkers most closely associated with postmodernism are Jean Baudrillard and Jean-François Lyotard.

Jean Baudrillard (1929–)

Jean Baudrillard is renowned for his critique of modern technology and media. He refuses to distinguish between appearances and any realities lying behind them. For him, the distinctions between signifier and signified have finally collapsed. Signs no longer refer to signifieds in any real sense. The world consists of 'floating signifiers'. These ideas he expounded in his work *Simulacra et Simulation* (1981). The notion of 'hyperreality' is born. Something is only real in the sense of the media in which it moves. Postmodern communication technologies generate free-floating images, and no one experiences anything other than in a derived form. A universal experience of the *banale* has come to replace any distinctive culture and the banality has only one accent: that of the United States of America.

His writings (for example, *Fatal Strategies*, *The Illusion of the End*) have become increasingly nihilistic: signs by their endless repetition and variation have become meaningless (one can think, for example, of the worldwide uses of the

Union Jack flag as an element in fashion design, in advertisements etc). The extremity of his views led him to the notorious statement, which attracted virulent criticism, that the Gulf War of 1991 was not real but a media event: 'it is unreal, war without the symptoms of war.' This has led many to suspect that Baudrillard himself has spun off into hyperreality and no longer inhabits an earthly body. In his arguments he considers no specific details of social or cultural contexts. It is not surprising that many of his ideas have featured prominently in science fiction writing and fantasy novels. Some have also argued that many of his ideas were prefigured in such works. Baudrillard himself has written an essay in praise of the science fiction writer J G Ballard. As already indicated his vision of the world has found many echoes in the cinema, especially in that genre of films in which virtual reality becomes indistinguishable from the real world, and also in the concept of the 'cyborg', a hybrid of technology and human being.

Jean-François Lyotard (1924–1998)

In his work *Discours, figure* (1971) Lyotard makes a distinction which he believed structuralism had ignored. He distinguishes between what is 'seen' and perceived in three dimensions (the 'figural') and what is 'read': the two-dimensional text. Echoing Foucault, he argues that what is regarded as rational thought by modernist thinkers is, in fact, a form of control and domination. For Lyotard, the 'figural' level, which seems to incorporate something akin to Freudian libido, or force of desire, acquires unified meaning by the operations of rational thought. Art, on the other hand, criticises and destabilises and works against any sense of completion and closure.

Perhaps Lyotard's most famous and influential work is *The Postmodern Condition* (1979). In this work, he argues that knowledge cannot claim to provide truth in any absolute sense, for it depends on 'language games' which are always related to specific contexts. Here Lyotard owes much to both Nietzsche and Wittgenstein. He claims that the Enlightenment goals of human liberation and the prevalence of reason produced only a kind of scientific hubris. Jürgen Habermas, for one, has refused to accept this assessment of the fate of Enlightenment goals and believes that they are still viable.

One implication of Lyotard's concept of postmodernism, which is important for the procedures adopted by literary criticism, is that analysis should proceed without any pre-set criteria. Ordering principles and rules are discovered in the process of analysis.

Sexual Orientation Theories

Specific sexual orientation theories (gay, lesbian and queer theories) have their roots in the Gay Liberation Movement in America in the late 1960s. Its aims were to counter discrimination against sexual minorities and to develop pride in homosexual identity. The word 'gay' has been preferred to 'homosexual' due to the latter word's pejorative associations.

Gay Theory

As with feminism, gay criticism and theory have undertaken to recover an alternative literary history, highlighting works, famous or otherwise, which have had either implicit or explicit gay themes. Also of interest has been how sexuality has been viewed and understood in past cultures, especially in those of Western Europe and America. Undoubtedly, the two main influences on gay theory have been the ideas of Sigmund Freud and Michel Foucault.

I. Sigmund Freud (1856–1939)

The central concerns of psychoanalysis have already been

outlined in the section devoted to that particular theoretical approach. Especially relevant to gay theory are Freud's *Three Essays on the Theory of Sexuality* (1905). Further pertinent works are various parts of the *Introductory Lectures on Psychoanalysis* (1916–17), and specific analyses in some of the case histories. Already in the essays of 1905 Freud asserted as given that not all men had a sexual interest in the opposite sex. Freud has been accused of setting up a normative approach to homosexuality: aiming to reintegrate the homosexual into society. But, in fact, he asserted on several occasions that, if a homosexual is happy with his condition, he should have no need of seeking psychoanalytic help. He only wished to help those who were not happy and wanted to reintegrate into the predominantly heterosexual society. Also important for gay theory is Freud's concept of 'polymorphous perversity': the idea that the young individual, male or female, is capable of all possible forms of sexual pleasure. The choice of sexual object is narrowed in the course of individual development.

II. Michel Foucault (1926–1984)

In *The History of Sexuality* (1976), Foucault argues that the concept of the 'homosexual' was born in the nineteenth century. Rather than being just a kind of behaviour involving specific acts (such as sodomy), 'the homosexual was now a species'. The homosexual acquired 'a case history, and a childhood' (see also the section on post-structuralism).

III. Alan Sinfield and Jonathan Dollimore

Alan Sinfield, in *Literature, Politics and Culture in Postwar Britain* (1976), analyses how effeminate behaviour has been used in literature as an indication of gay sexuality, often with negative connotations. Together with Jonathan Dollimore, he also analysed concepts of masculinity in the works of Shakespeare. In *Sexual Dissidence* (1991), Dollimore explored the relationship between power and sexuality and the possibility of what is labelled as perverse becoming a politically subversive force. For him, as for Foucault, the naming of something as perverse enables authority to control it: 'Perversion is the product and vehicle of power, a construction which enables it to gain a purchase within the realm of the psychosexual: authority legitimates itself by fastening upon discursively constructed, sexually perverse identities of its own making.'

Lesbian Theory

Lesbian Theory is clearly allied with feminism in its concern about the suppression of women. But it sees heterosexuality as a norm which helps maintain a patriarchal social system. Gayle Rubin coined the term 'compulsory heterosexuality' to explain how heterosexuality was an imposed norm rather than a natural condition.

A central problem for lesbian theory is identifying what constitutes a lesbian text. Maggie Humm raised the essential questions in *Practising Feminist Criticism: An Introduction* (1995): 'Are texts lesbian if neither author nor content are *explicitly* lesbian? How much of a text has to be about lesbianism to be regarded as lesbian?' Lesbian theory has, it would appear, explored all possible areas of lesbian perspectives on literature, including those which it shares with gay theory. One approach has been to develop lesbian reading strategies: how to read a text from a lesbian point of view. There is naturally the danger of serious misreadings with this approach. How far is one prepared to go along with Adrienne Rich's lesbian reading of Charlotte Brontë's *Jane Eyre* (*The Temptations of a Motherless Girl*, 1980). It focuses on the way in which Jane Eyre is brought up by various substitute mothers or female mentors. The heterosexual romance is seen as essentially a socially imposed construct.

Important for the identification of a lesbian literary tradition is Jane Rule's *Lesbian Images* (1975). She analyses the works of some twentieth century lesbian writers, including Gertrude Stein, Ivy Compton-Burnett and others. Another approach is to explore literature as encoded accounts of lesbianism. This involves both analysing obscure idioms as well as analysing idioms obscurely, and drawing attention to gender ambiguities. An example of this kind of study is Catherine Stimpson's *Where the Meanings Are: Feminism and Cultural Spaces* (1988).

Queer Theory

The term 'queer' used to be a pejorative term for a homo-sexual person or perverse behaviour. In the 1990s it was taken up by a new mode of sexual theory with a proud determination to give it a forceful edge. Queer theory is also greatly indebted to postmodern and gay and lesbian thought. It broadens the whole basis of theory related to sexual orientation, and is concerned very much with the notion of difference and marginal identity. It has also become an umbrella term because of the emergence of other foci which do not fit easily into the categories of 'gay' or 'lesbian', such as transvestism, bisexuality etc. In queer theory, there is a definite tendency to disrupt all kinds of fixed categorisation and to challenge all attempts at analysing sexuality in terms of binary oppositions. Variety and deviance is celebrated. Hans Bertens has summed up well the relation of queer theory to literary analysis: 'Queer theory's contribution to literary and cultural studies lies in its emphasis on sexuality as a fourth category of analysis – next to race, gender and class – and in its insistence that sexuality and gender cannot very well be separated.' (*Literary Theory*, 1992).

Judith Butler

The American critic Judith Butler, in an essay entitled *Imitation and Gender Insubordination* (1991), uses the word 'queer' as in the sense of the idiom 'to queer someone's pitch' (spoil or ruin a plan). She sees the essential function of queer theory to be to thwart, disrupt and generally make certain things impossible, whether it be prevailing ideologies or sexual stereotypes. In the same work, she is concerned to deconstruct the notion of fixed personal identity. She believes the 'I' appears to be a fixed identity only because we repeat it so many times. So also, she says, sexual orientation might be the result of repetition of specific acts. We have only the illusion of being a coherent person with a coherent sexual identity. This means that heterosexuality is also the effect of a string of performances. Heterosexual, or gay, or lesbian acts are copies of which there are no originals: 'Like gender, sexuality is a social construction.' This also helps to explain the interest of queer theorists in drag and cross-dressing. Such acts are not due to inherent tendencies but are the results of conscious choices. They make clear and visible the contradictions in a heterosexually dominated world.

Eve Kosovsky Sedgwick

In her book, *Epistemology of the Closet* (1991), Sedgwick pursues the political implications of queer theory more forcefully than Butler. (She also takes an anthropological perspective, showing how homosexual rites and cross-dressing in other cultures have been misunderstood by projecting First World categories onto Third World cultures.) Another of her arguments is that the distinction 'heterosexual/homosexual' has had profound effects on modern modes of thought: 'it has affected our culture through its ineffaceable marking'. She then proceeds to list a large number of binary oppositions characterising modern western societies, which she believes are direct results of the 'heterosexual/homosexual' distinction, for example 'secrecy/disclosure', 'innocence/initiation', 'discipline/terrorism', 'active/passive', 'art/kitsch' etc.

Ethnic Theory

One of the aims of an ethnically aware critical theory has been to break down notions of fixed racial and ethnic identities, even where there are apparently marked distinctions. While breaking them down, the distinction between race and ethnicity has nevertheless been retained. Race relates more to genetically inherited characteristics and ethnicity is more concerned with shared cultural identity. The concern has also been to understand relationships between these concepts and other commonly employed concepts in cultural theory and, especially, in postcolonial theory. The main body of work to date has been in the area of black culture. French-speaking black writers started to use the concept of *négritude* (negroness). The term can be loosely defined as attitudes to the world and nature and modes of thought common among black races. Other racial and ethnic groups have yet to have extensive studies devoted to them.

Henry Louis Gates Jr. (1950–)

In *'Race', Writing and Difference* (1985) and other articles, Henry Louis Gates Jr expresses the belief that it is not sufficient to apply critical categories developed in relation to white western literature to the literature of black communities: '...we must turn to the black tradition itself to develop theories of criticism indigenous to our cultures.' He also argues for the breakdown of the binary opposition of 'black' and 'white': 'We are all ethnics', and we all have to transcend the conditions of our ethnically bound perceptions.

Stuart Hall (1932–)

In various articles, including *Minimal Selves* (1988) and *Cultural Identity and Diaspora* (1990), Stuart Hall has used the term 'hybridity', borrowed from postcolonial theory, to describe the experience of African races, which have spread into other cultures and ethnic areas (diaspora). For Hall the people of such a diaspora have not retained any racial purity but have necessarily become diverse, or 'hybrid'. He has also developed the notion of a 'diaspora aesthetic' to analyse the art and literature of such hybrid existence.

Paul Gilroy

Paul Gilroy, in his book *The Black Atlantic: Modernity and Double Consciousness* (1993), stresses the 'double consciousness' of the black experience: the consciousness of black people is divided between that of their original culture and the contemporary British or American culture (in the instances examined). Critics of literature by black writers must consider this 'double consciousness' in their evaluations.

Black Feminist Theory

Writers such as Barbara Smith and bell hooks (sic) have expanded the basis of ethnic studies, by raising awareness of the status of black women writers in general and of black lesbian writers in particular. June Jordan, Paula Gunn Allen and others have also written extensively of the literary experience of Native American and Asian American women writers.

Recent Trends

There seems to be a general feeling among many theorists that the whole era of theory, or its heyday at least, may be over. Recent titles indicate that this feeling is broadly based. There are, for example, the collection of essays edited by Martin McQuillan and others called *Post-Theory: New Directions in Criticism* (1999) and two works with the same title *After Theory*, one by Thomas Docherty and the other by Terry Eagleton (both published in 2003). Some theorists have decided that it is high time critics returned to detailed analysis of literary texts. Jonathan Culler, in an essay in *What's Left of Theory?* (2000), has argued that it is time to 'reground the literary in litera-ture', and Valentine Cunningham, in *Reading After Theory* (2002), calls for a return to traditional close reading of texts. But Terry Eagleton has argued, in *After Theory* (2003), that cultural theory, and by implication literary theory, has always read its texts closely. Despite there being apparent disarray in theoretical stances and a lack of forceful new directions, some concerns have crystallised into distinctive trends, which can be identified and, indeed, named.

New Historicism

A useful working definition of new historicism is provided by John Brannigan in *New Historicism and Cultural Materialism* (1998). He describes new historicism as 'a mode of critical interpretation which privileges power relations as the most important context for texts of all kinds', and '...it treats literary texts as a space where power relations are made visible'. The power referred to here is, of course, that posited by Foucault which is exerted though discourses, allowing the subject to believe that he or she is free and able to make autonomous decisions. The historical period of a text has to be studied in detail to determine what power relations (or, in Foucault's terms, which discursive practices) were operating and how they affected the text. New historicism seeks its evidence anywhere, not only in the text. Everything which constitutes part of a culture can be analysed like a text. Intertextuality (tracing relations between texts) is therefore a primary focus. Terry Eagleton has aptly written: '...the new historicism was prepared in pluralist spirit to examine any topic at all as long as it cropped up somewhere in the works of Michel Foucault' (*Literary Theory*, Eagleton 2002).

A leading practitioner, Stephen Greenblatt, in his book *Resonance and Wonder* (1990), argues that 'new historicism, as I understand it, does not posit historical processes as unalterable and inexorable, but it does tend to discover limits or constraints upon individual intervention...' A major criticism levelled against new historicism is that its practitioners are blind to the conditions affecting their own perspectives. To some extent, their arguments are always the products of their own personal and social situation and can never attain the kind of objectivity which they seem to expect.

The new historicists have produced a large body of critical analyses focused on Romantic and Renaissance literature especially. They have explored, for example, the ways in which Shakespeare's plays act out the power structure of the Tudor monarchy, reflecting the discourses dominating contemporary society. Although subversive ideas are frequently explored in Shakespeare's plays, these ideas are always contained within the controlling discourses of the era. They do not become revolutionary. The critic Marjorie Levinson sees a work in the context of its time and related to the dominant discourses, but not necessarily as its contemporaries or its author viewed it: the aim is 'to know a work as neither it, nor its original readers, nor its author could know it' (*Wordsworth's Great Period Poems*, 1986).

Cultural Materialism

Cultural materialism was developed in Great Britain as a politically more radical form of new historicism. For them Foucault's ideas imply greater instability in the power structures of discourses than the new historicists perceive. They base their more dynamic model of culture on the ideas of Raymond Williams, as formulated way back in 1977 (in *Marxism and Literature*). Eagleton has defined the cultural materialism conceived by Williams as 'a form of analysis which examined culture less as a set of isolated artistic monuments than as a material formation' complete with its own 'identifiable audiences, historically conditioned thought-forms' etc. For Eagleton, cultural materialism also forms a kind of bridge between Marxism and postmodernism and, like new historicism, takes on board a wide range of topics, including feminism, sexual orientation, ethnic and postcolonial issues. Another focus of interest (as in some writings by Jonathan Dollimore and Alan Sinfield) is the ways in which literature from the past has functioned and been perceived in later periods. Sinfield has also explored his notion of 'faultlines' in literature, or the contradictions in the ideologies discoverable in texts. And Michael Bristol has taken up Bakhtin's concept of 'carnival' and applied it to Renaissance culture in England. Carnival is the prime example of how popular culture can exist in opposition to officialdom. Carnival, Bristol claims, also mocks the symbols of power, although the criticism has been levelled against his argument that carnival cannot be an effective opposition strategy because it is, in fact, no more than sanctioned mockery. It is only an outlet for frustration and has had its sting removed.

Genetic Criticism

Genetic criticism seeks demonstrable textual evidence for an author's intentions and analyses the factors determining the nature of the final text as it progresses from manuscript to book. It also examines the effects of censorship and revision. It attempts to define precisely what can be legitimately said about a text. The critic Jean-Michel

Rabaté is closely associated with the formulation of the principles governing its practices.

New Aestheticism

The name was coined by John Joughlin and Simon Malpas in *The New Aestheticism* (2003). The thrust of their argument is that developments in cultural theory have led to the loss of the very notion of a 'work of art'. Critics no longer respect 'the sense of art's specificity as an object of analysis...' The critics supporting the new aesthetics do not call for a return to a kind of 'art for art's sake' approach but assert that they wish to relate a new sense of aesthetic form to an awareness of social context and political concerns. John Brenkman in *Extreme Criticism* (2000), has called for closer study of the relationship between inner form and the worldliness of a text. In *The Radical Aesthetic* (2000) Isobel Armstrong argues for establishing a 'democratic aesthetic', which she believes possible because we all share common components of the aesthetic life such as playing and dreaming. Thomas Docherty, in his book *After Theory* (1997), introduced a new approach to the role of literature in education and culture in general. In the theory of the new aesthetics, popularity and accessibility would seem to be implicit if not explicit watchwords. Its exponents are high on ideals couched in fine sounding words. It remains to be seen whether a coherent body of critical theory supporting these ideals will emerge.

Ecocriticism

In an edition of *The Guardian* (30 July 2005), an article by the writer Robert Macfarlane appeared under the title 'Where the Wild Things Are'. The front page of the 'Review' section showed a portrait of him with the heading 'The Landscape Library: Robert Macfarlane on Ecoclassics'. In the article, Macfarlane argues for a whole new perspective on the concerns on which literature and literary study should be focusing. In an earlier essay, he had proposed the setting up and publication of a library of classics of nature writing from Britain and Ireland: '…it would be a series of local writings, which concentrated on particular places, and which worked always to individuate, never to generalise.' Any book, in order to be included, would 'have to evince the belief that the fate of humanity and the fate of nature are inseparable'. And the natural environment would have to be approached 'not with a view to conquest, acquisition and short-term use, but according to the principles of restraint and reciprocity.' Macfarlane has essentially started the process of establishing a canon of ecologically aware British literature, which can serve as the basis of an ecocritical approach to the study of literature.

In America the concept of 'ecocriticism' can be traced back at least as far as an essay by William Rueckert in 1978, called *Literature and Ecology: An Experiment in Ecocriticism*. The concept lay dormant for some time until Cheryll Burgess Glotfelty reawakened interest in the project by publishing a survey of the field, which she edited with Harold Fromm under the title *The Ecocriticism*

Reader: Landmarks in Literary Ecology (1996). In 1992 the Association for the Study of Literature and Environment (ASLE) was founded, with its own journal, newsletter and website. There still seems to be no clear agreement as to what exactly constitutes 'ecocriticism'. Some scholars have claimed that it adds the new category of 'place' to those of race, class, gender etc, as perspectives for analysing literature. The critic Lawrence Buell has argued that in theory there has for too long been 'a gap between texts and facts'. Ecocriticism fills that gap: 'Ecocriticism assumes that there is an extra-textual reality that impacts human beings and their artefacts – and vice versa.' Glen A Love (University of Oregon) has said: 'It's time to heal the breach between the hard sciences and the humanities – and literary theory isn't going to do it.' Some essays in *The Ecocriticism Reader*, however, argue that the theories of Foucault and Said are relevant to a study of the environment which is itself a cultural construct.

In the introduction to the same volume Glotfelty and Fromm define ecocriticism as 'the study of the relationship between literature and the physical environment'. Ecocritics ask such questions as: 'How is nature represented in this sonnet? What role does the physical setting play in the plot of this novel? Are the values expressed in this play consistent with ecological wisdom?' etc. Another question considered is 'Do men write about nature differently than women do?' Not surprisingly, this has led to a sub-category of ecocriticism known as 'ecofeminism' with its own anthologies of women nature writers. Louise H Westling of the University of Oregon is, however, concerned about how ecofeminism emphasises the way gender is reflected in depictions of landscape and believes that it reinforces the tradition of assuming that the earth is female and those who use and dominate it male: 'The land is not a woman. But from ancient times, writers have used feminine images to justify conquering it.'

Theory and After

There are some advantages in writing about an extensive topic within the scope of a limited number of words. Rather like imminent death, it concentrates the mind wonderfully. It forces one to pose questions about fundamental assumptions and focus on essential principles. The endless word-spin and obsessive pursuit of ramifications for arguments have to be pruned, brutally if necessary, leaving often a very rough hewn trunk. But, if it is vigorous and viable, the trunk will survive. Feeble saplings I have left quite deliberately exposed in their frailty to the elements: these elements being any future critical appraisals in literary theory and vagaries in the climate of public opinion.

Within the major sections, designated by schools of thought, it is noticeable that most subheadings refer to specific writers by name. This was intended partly for the convenience of the reader, in tracking down individual theorists, but it also reveals a general truth about the nature of literary theory: it is characterised by many different systems of terminology and categorisation. While there are commonly employed terms (eg metaphor, metonymy, signifier, signified, text, binary opposites etc), many theorists have chosen to reformulate the concepts of

141

other theorists in their own terms, sometimes with little change of meaning, but at other times clearly indicating a more extensive application or somewhat different perspective. The lack of agreement on terminology has doubtless been one of the reasons for the failure to formulate a unified theory. The term 'theory' has come to refer in fact to a particular theorist's 'way of talking' about something. This returns us to the challenge which all theories must face, and which I outlined in my introductory chapter: can it be proved or disproved?

The Validity of Interpretation

An interpretation may fit the facts but does that make it correct or legitimate? Many poststructuralist and deconstructive critics would argue that this does not matter anyway: all readings are 'misreadings'. But this mode of thought leads only to incoherent nihilism and benefits nobody: all judgements are considered possible because relative and therefore permissible.

Even if it is accepted that literary theory can never aspire to being scientific, and granting that much theory in the natural and social sciences is, in any case, built upon insecure hypotheses, it is still useful to apply Karl Popper's 'falsifiability' test in assessing the application of a theory. In proposing an interpretation of any element in a literary text or other form of discourse, it is still necessary to cite evidence from some related source, internal or external to the text, to prove or at least demonstrate the likelihood of the validity of the interpretation. If the way in which the theory is formulated precludes the possibility of citing pertinent evidence, then it is not a valid theory. Claiming that the nursery rhyme *Little Miss Muffet* is an account of an invasion by eight-legged aliens gets us nowhere without some internal textual or external evidence. What counts as evidence depends, of course, on what one is looking for in the text.

It may well be that nowadays most theorists agree that no final all-embracing interpretation of any text is ever possible in any conceivable context: that you can never discover exactly what it meant to its original author, to his/her contemporary readers or to any subsequent generations. But judgements have to be made. Granted the impossibility of any absolute judgements, we all still have to make practical judgements to manage experience and give some purpose to our pursuits. And, with cautious critical testing of evidence defined according to the hypotheses assumed, it is possible to acquire extensive if not absolute understanding of most literary texts. One goes as far as the text and internal as well as external evidence will allow. In the words of Jonathan Culler: 'What drives theory, after all, is the desire to see how far an idea or argument can go and to question alternative accounts and their presuppositions.'

Some Fundamental Issues

In reading through my survey again, it became obvious that there are certain issues, concerns, problem areas (call them what you will) which recur in various guises throughout, and which relate to what one might term fundamental matters, of which most (if not necessarily all) theories of literature have to provide some account. There are at least eight such fundamental 'issues' which can be clearly identified:

i. Authorial Presence

How does one take into consideration the role of the author as producer of a text, if at all? How is the author's identity present in the text? Is the narrator assumed to be the author, an imaginary being, or a character in the story? Is the narrator reliable?

ii. The Text and the World

Is the text assumed to reflect the real world in some way? If so, is this achieved through naïve realism or through self-conscious artifice? Is an attempt made to analyse the text in isolation from the world in which it was produced and/or the world which the reader inhabits? Or is the text analysed as part of a continuum with worlds in which it exists?

iii. Alienation

To what extent does the text incorporate devices of alienation, or 'defamiliarisation'? Is the particular theoretical approach being employed concerned to raise awareness of such devices? What is the nature of the forms of alienation being considered?

iv. Mode of Textual Analysis

How does the particular theoretical approach analyse the actual text on the page? Does it consider inner contradictions and paradoxes? Does it explore binary oppositions? Does it attempt to relate all of the parts to the whole? Does it consider the handling of grammar and syntax? Is it essentially formalist or does it attempt to consider factors outside the actual text?

v. Interpretation

Does the particular theoretical approach assume the possibility of only a limited interpretation or does it accept that any interpretation is unlimited? How, if at all, can specific interpretations be validated? Does the interpretation involve establishing a 'hermeneutic circle', with each part of the interpretation confirming the others? Is this circle in fact a 'vicious' one, providing only internal consistency?

vi. Perspectives

Does the particular theoretical approach bring a specific perspective to the text, viewing it in the light of special concerns or interests? Examples of such perspectives are: feminism, gay theory, ethnic concerns, socialist/Marxist thought, psychoanalysis etc.

vii. Reading Against the Grain

Does the particular theoretical approach attempt to read

the text in an unconventional way, subverting normal conventions of grammar, reading and assumptions about form etc? This occurs in the deliberate 'misreadings' provided by some poststructuralists and in deconstructive approaches.

viii Aesthetic Judgement

Does the particular theoretical approach attempt to evaluate a literary text as 'good' or 'bad' in any way? Is any form of aesthetic judgement provided or implied? Is there any consideration of specifically literary characteristics of the text?

These are essentially the main parameters within which the theories outlined in this book operate. Each of the schools of thought will answer the questions in different ways and some reject their relevance. I propose them merely as a useful mode of comparing the suppositions and concerns of the various theoretical approaches and methods of analysis.

Negotiating Meaning

There is no need to take up the extreme stances concerning the interpretability of texts implied by many post-structural, deconstructive and postmodernist critics. Meaning may, indeed, be indefinitely deferred. But this is no reason to give up the act of interpretation in despair. Language works. We use it every day effectively. Writers communicate. We understand and value their words, even if we do not understand every single point they make. In conversation we understand each other by *negotiating* meaning: we ask each other to clarify, provide examples etc. Does anything similar occur in the act of reading? Even in reading a contemporary literary work we always grasp only partially what the text is communicating. We seek confirmation of our interpretation in our knowledge of linguistic usage and, if necessary, by consulting other contemporary sources (other people, a dictionary, the media, not to mention what we know of the author's ways of thinking from other sources, etc). Reading a literary work from the past is clearly only different by degree not in kind. Accepting that all judgements are relative is not a 'cop out', not an avoidance of judgement nor of commitment to interpretation (or it should not be). It is rather an undeniable characteristic of all knowledge. Neglect the fact at your peril. Some theorists, while willing to grant that there are imperfections in a text, assume nevertheless the existence of an ideally perfect reader or critic. Most real readers and critics never quite come up to scratch. Where would critics be if they had no other imperfect critics to criticise?

It seems to me a good working hypothesis to assume that, when a literary work is created and published, it enters into a world of eternal flux. It may not appear so to the writer and reader at the time but language, thought and social reality are in a process of constant change. What seemed to be a valid interpretation last year may not seem so now. The Greek philosopher Heracleitus asserted that one cannot step into the same river twice (what he is actually reported to have said is 'Upon those who step into the same rivers different and ever different waters flow down'). It must however be a first step to ascertain the most likely meanings for the original author of a text, for its first readers and its relation to the world in which it was created, however imperfect this knowledge must of necessity be. Then one can start to analyse how perceptions have changed with time and attempt to interpret the text in the light of whatever perspective takes one's fancy.

The Rebirth of the Author

At least since the highly influential essay by the two New Critics W K Wimsatt and Monroe C Beardsley, entitled *The Intentional Fallacy* (1949), in which they criticise the tendency to confuse what the author intended in the writing of a work with what is actually there on the page, critics have only very self-consciously and gingerly referred to an author's intentions in his work. And, after the publication of Barthes' essay *The Death of the Author*, it became almost heresy to bring up the topic. Yet authors, readers, TV documentaries and critics continue to talk freely of author's intentions. Has the wheel come full circle? The metaphor is not the most apt. The German Expressionist writer Kasimir Edschmid used the image of a spiral to illustrate how experience changes but passes over the same points again and again. It is no longer possible to talk of the paramountcy of an author's intentions but it would be folly to exclude them from consideration altogether. After all, it is possible to make some valid statements about an author's intentions, even from the text alone: the intentions are often indicated by the sheer choice of material, together with uses of metaphor, metonymy and, especially, in the uses of irony and sarcasm. Is it after all possible to read Charles Dickens' *A Christmas Carol* without understanding that Dickens' intentions were to make the reader aware of the corrupting influence of capitalism and its values and the plight of the poor? Most writers would throw in the towel, if all they could expect in response to their work was constant misreadings. It is high time, it seems to me, for a reassessment of the writer's role in the literary process. Derrida wrote of there being a greater sense of being at one with the self when speaking than when writing. Yet many writers write because they feel their situation to be the reverse: they only feel at one with themselves when writing. And Foucault argued that the writer often denies his or her own presence in writing. This may be a necessary or desired illusion but surely no writer nor reader ever truly believes in the absence of an author. Wayne C. Booth drew attention to the difference between the actual author and the authorial voice (the narrator as a named or an unnamed character in the text), but this distinction is not always unbridgeable. It is possible sometimes, admittedly not always, to establish points of identity between the actual author and the authorial voice.

Problems of Evaluation

The question whether a work of literature is 'good' or 'bad' will probably always remain a vexed one, as will the question about what distinguishes a literary text from a non-literary text. The Russian semiotician Yury Lotman argued that literary texts are more worthy of our attention than non-literary texts, because they carry a 'higher information load'. A good poem was for him 'semantically saturated', while a poor poem carried insufficient information. This is clearly an inadequate yardstick for judging works of literature in general. A short simple poem can be more highly regarded than a long complex one. There is a long list of characteristics which one attributes to a work, including what intellectual and emotional effects it has on the reader and how it relates to our understanding of the world from which it originated as well as to the world in which we exist. We consider all these factors before having the confidence to declare the work 'good' or 'bad'.

The Future of Literary Theory

Whether the heyday of literary theory is over, as some suspect, or whether there is just a hiatus while theorists consider which hobby-horses to leap onto next, it does seem likely that, in some form or other, critics will continue to theorise about literature and methods of analysing it. Terry Eagleton has suggested that the way forward may be to return to a reconsideration of origins and to reformulate for the modern world a theory of 'poetics', indeed of 'rhetoric', as first expounded by Aristotle. Doubtless specific interest groups will continue to propose new angles on literary studies, all very interesting and revealing, if essentially providing only partial perspectives of literary texts. We have had Marxist, psychoanalytic, lesbian, gay, postcolonial, ethnic, ecocritical perspectives. There is no reason why we should not have more approaches, all of them equally legitimate.

With only the gentlest irony intended, I end this survey with several I have dreamed up myself. Think of the insights we would gain through the application of gastronomic critical theory (the roles of meals, eating and drinking, diets and the like in literature, and why have some writers repressed details of meals in their writing while others have glorified them?). Built environment theory would also yield much about human treatment of the material world. And should not children's rights be getting a look in? Not to mention ageism (prejudice against people of specific ages, not just the oldies). Is it not high time we had an ageist study of Shakespeare's *King Lear* and an analysis of attitudes to the various generations in Galsworthy's *The Forsyte Saga*? My personal favourite, which I am seriously thinking of inaugurating, is cynocriticism which will raise awareness of the treatment and significance of dogs in literature. Too long has the significance of the poodle in Goethe's *Faust* been overlooked, as has the presence of the little dog in Chekhov's *The Lady with the Little Dog* and the eponymous creature in Simenon's *The Yellow Dog*. In Conan Doyle's *Silver Blaze,* Sherlock Holmes would never have solved the crime if had not been for 'the curious incident of the dog in the night-time'. By remaining silent, the dog communicated to Holmes the identity of the criminal. In many works by writers who are deemed among the greatest, dogs behave in ways which put human morality and faithfulness to shame. Bill Sykes' dog, in *Oliver Twist*, reveals his heart to be in the right place even if his master's is not.

Reference Materials

In general the works included are listed in order of general usefulness and accessibility to the complete beginner, with the most accessible listed first in each category. The works also contain especially useful bibliographies to guide the student in further reading.

General surveys

Selden, R., Widdowson, P. and Brooker, P., *A Reader's Guide to Contemporary Literary Theory*, London and New York, etc., Pearson Longman, 2005 (first published 1985).

Bertens, Hans, *Literary Theory: The Basics*, London and New York, Routledge, 2001.

Eagleton, Terry, *Literary Theory: An Introduction*, Oxford, Blackwell, 2nd. Edition, 2002 (First published 1983).

Bennett, Andrew and Royle, Nicholas, *Introduction to Literature, Criticism and Theory*, London and New York, Pearson Longman, 2004 (first edition 1995).

Anthologies of Literary Theory

Lodge, David (ed.), *Modern Criticism and Theory: A Reader*,

London and New York, Longman, 1990 (first published 1988).

Rivkin, Julie and Ryan, Michael, *Literary Theory: An Anthology*, Oxford, Blackwell, 2004 (first published 1998).

Rice, Philip and Waugh, Patricia, *Modern Literary Theory: A Reader*, London and New York, Arnold/Oxford University Press, 1989.

Broadly Based Reflections

Culler, Jonathan, *Literary Theory: A Very Short Introduction*, Oxford, Oxford University Press, 1997.

Eagleton, Terry, *After Theory*, London, Penguin, 2004 (first published 2003).

General Reference

Cuddon, J A (revised by Preston, C.E.), *Dictionary of Literary Terms*, London, Penguin Reference, 1999 (first published in 1977).

Macey, David, *Dictionary of Critical Theory*, London, Penguin Reference, 2001, (first edition 2000).

Index